THE WAY TO
PENTECOST

THE WAY TO
PENTECOST

Samuel Chadwick

former principal,
Cliff College, Sheffield, England

CLC ❖ PUBLICATIONS
Fort Washington, Pennsylvania 19034

Published by CLC ✦ Publications

U.S.A.
P.O. Box 1449, Fort Washington, PA 19034

GREAT BRITAIN
51 The Dean, Alresford, Hants. SO24 9BJ

AUSTRALIA
P.O. Box 419M, Manunda, QLD 4879

NEW ZEALAND
10 MacArthur Street, Feilding

ISBN 0-87508-579-2

First published in Great Britain in 1932
by Hodder and Stoughton Limited.

Copyright © 2000 Cliff College, Sheffield, England

This reset edition under special arrangement
with Cliff College, Sheffield, England.

This printing 2001

Printed in the United States of America

Contents

About the Author

Preacher burns his sermons—
then catches fire himself!

SAMUEL CHADWICK was zealous for Jesus, but God had more in store for him: the power of the Holy Spirit's fire!

Samuel Chadwick was born in the industrial north of England in 1860. His father worked long hours in the cotton mill, and when he was only eight Samuel went to work there too, as a means of supporting the impoverished family.

Devout Methodists, they attended chapel three times on Sunday, and as a young boy Chadwick gave his heart to Christ. Listening to God's Word week by week, he often felt the inner call to serve Christ. It seemed impossible, as he was poor and uneducated; but in faith he made preparations. After a twelve-hour factory shift he would rush home for five hours of prayer and study.

At the age of 21 he was appointed lay pastor of a chapel at Stacksteads, Lancashire. It was no dream appointment; the congregation was self-satisfied. Yet Chadwick threw himself in with great optimism. He had been trained to prepare well-researched and interesting sermons as the sure way to bring in the crowds. He recalled later: "This led unconsciously to a false aim in my work. I lived and labored for my sermons, and was unfortunately more concerned about their excellence and reputation than the repentance of the people."

Soon, however, his sermons were exhausted and nothing had changed. Staring defeat in the face and sensing his lack of real power, he felt an intense hunger kindled within him for more of God. At this point he heard the testimony of someone who had been revitalized by an experience of the Holy Spirit, so with a few friends he covenanted to pray and search the Scriptures until God sent revival.

One evening as he was praying over his next sermon, a powerful sense of conviction settled on him. His pride, blindness and reliance on human methods paraded before his eyes as God humbled him to the dust. Well into the night he wrestled and repented, then he got out his pile of precious sermons and set fire to them! The result was immediate: the Holy Spirit fell upon him. In his own words: "I could not explain what had happened, but it was a bigger thing than I had ever known. There came into my soul a deep peace, a thrilling joy, and a new sense of power. My mind was quickened. I felt I had received a new faculty of understanding. Every power was vitalized. My body was quickened. There was a new sense of spring and vitality, a new power of endurance, and a strong man's exhilaration in big things."

The tide turned. At his next sermon seven souls were converted ("one for each of my barren years"), and he called the whole congregation to a week of prayer. The following weekend most of the church was baptized in the Holy Spirit and revival began to spread through the valleys. In the space of a few months hundreds were converted to Jesus, among them some of the most notorious sinners in the area.

The pattern was repeated over the next few years as Chadwick moved to various places. 1890 saw him in Leeds, where the power of God was so strongly upon him that the chapel was full half an hour before the service began, and police had to control the crowds. The river of God moved strongly, and Chadwick records: "We were always praying and fighting [the devil], singing and rejoicing, doing the impossible and planning still bigger things. The newspapers never left us alone, and people came from far and wide."

Opposition was swept away and within a few years the chapel had to be demolished and a substantial church built.

Always a man of the people, Chadwick would spend his Saturdays mixing with local workers. Once, when his wife was away, he teasingly invited anyone who was lonely to come for Saturday tea. He expected about a dozen. Six hundred turned up! Yet God had catered: one church member was a baker and had been awakened by the Lord with the order to bake for all he was worth!

The final phase of Chadwick's life was spent as Principal of Cliff College, a Methodist training school for preachers, and it was here that he wrote his famous book *The Way to Pentecost*, which was being printed when he died in 1932. In it we read: "I owe everything to the gift of Pentecost. For fifty days the facts of the gospel were complete, but no conversions were recorded. Pentecost registered three thousand souls. It is by fire that a holy passion is kindled in the soul, whereby we live the life of God. The soul's safety is in its heat. Truth without enthusiasm, morality without emotion, ritual without soul, make for a Church without power."

"Destitute of the Fire of God, nothing else counts; possessing Fire, nothing else matters."

Foreword

"GOOD wine needs no bush," and such excellent wine as this volume contains wants no commendation. But my old friend expressed a strong desire that I should write a Foreword. And I would rather be thought presumptuous than disloyal to his behest.

A pathetic interest attaches to these pages. While they were still in the press their author passed on to his great reward. The book may, therefore, be regarded as in some way a memorial volume. In subject and content it is worthy of such designation. Throughout his ministry Mr. Chadwick has given exceptional prominence to the doctrine of the Holy Spirit: The Lord and Giver of Life, both to the Church which is Christ's body and to every member of that body; who spoke by the prophets and is the flaming tongue impelling each believer to speak that which he has felt and seen.

Some excellent books of recent years have done something to remove the reproach given in chapter one, that there has been no great work on the Holy Spirit since 1674. Mr. Chadwick might have been

Owen's successor, but this volume is not the book he would then have written. It is not a formal treatise at all, but a selection from articles on the subject which appeared from time to time in *Joyful News*. Each chapter is therefore complete in itself and more or less independent of the remainder. Mr. Chadwick was not even responsible for the selection, which has been made by Rev. J. I. Brice, his son in the gospel. The editor has shown much judgment in his task and has succeeded in giving us a book with more than a mere appearance of unity.

In a collection having such an origin some repetition of idea and illustration is inevitable. But the book gives a powerful presentation of the teaching of Scripture from the practical side. It has the characteristic mark of the author: full and accurate knowledge of the Scriptures, clearness of teaching, precision of statement, depth of insight and practical purpose. It cannot fail to improve the mind, quicken the conscience and kindle earnest desire to receive the gift of the Spirit in its fullness.

As in *The Path of Prayer*, Mr. Chadwick does not hesitate to share with the reader some of the great moments of personal experience. To sit at the feet of one whose ear the Lord has wakened, to whom He also has given the tongue of the learned, is no ordinary boon. To all, whether weary or eager, who take that submissive position, I confidently predict the hearing of a word in season.

F. L. Wiseman

1

Do We Believe in
the Holy Ghost?

THE APOSTLES' Creed
contains ten articles on the
Person and Work of Christ and only one on the Holy
Spirit. The proportion of ten to one about represents
the interest in the doctrine of the Spirit in the history
of Christian thought. No doctrine of the Christian faith
has been so neglected. Sermons and hymns are
singularly barren on this subject, and the last great
book on the Spirit was written in 1674. This is all the
more remarkable when we remember that the Holy
Spirit is the ultimate fact of revelation and the unique
force in redemption. No other religion has anything
corresponding to the Christian doctrine of the Spirit,
and in the Christian religion there is nothing so vital,
pervasive, and effective. John Owen speaks of it as the
touchstone of faith: the one article by which the
Church stands or falls. Thomas Arnold said it is "the
very main thing of all. We are living under the
dispensation of the Spirit; in that character God now

reveals Himself to His people. He who does not know God the Holy Ghost cannot know God at all."

The Holy Scriptures declare Him to be the revealer of all truth, the active agent in all works of redemption, and from first to last the instrument of grace in the experience of salvation. In Him, and through Him, and by Him, is the power that saves. Illumination and conviction, repentance and regeneration, assurance and sanctification, are all the work of God the eternal Spirit. To the Church He is the Source and Supply of wisdom and power. The Church is the Body of Christ, indwelt and controlled by the Spirit. He directs, energizes, and controls. From first to last, this dispensation is the dispensation of the Spirit.

The Fruit of Neglect

The Church affirms its faith in the Holy Ghost every time it repeats its Creed, but does the Church really believe its belief? Modern writers are contending that the name is nothing more than a figure of speech for "spiritual atmosphere." They regard it as one of the misfortunes of the Christian religion that personality has been claimed for the Spirit. The life of the Church witnesses to the same attitude. The things of the Spirit are ignored as of no account. Atmosphere is valued. Religious assemblies of a certain order give a large place to silent pauses which produce emotional excitement. When our fathers glowed with fires kindled in the soul, they gave vent in noise; the modern way is to be still. Spirituality and silence are as wedded as were revivalism and rowdiness. Both types are emotional, but revivalists did believe their work was of the Spirit; the Quietists cultivate psychological influence. They speak of the Spirit with a different content from that of the Creeds.

The blunders and disasters of the Church are largely, if not entirely, accounted for by the neglect of the Spirit's ministry and mission. The morass of speculation about the Bible takes no account of the Holy Spirit. It regards inspiration as negligible, and insists upon interpreting revealed truth by standards no different from those for history and literature. Miracles are condemned without trial. Prophecy is dismissed without inquiry. Revelation is ignored without reason. Under the plea of breadth, all truth is thrust into uniform ruts. Our Lord spoke of the Spirit as the Spirit of Truth, and promised that He would guide His people into all truth. He spoke by the prophets. There were many writers, but He is the Author, and the Bible can neither be accounted for nor interpreted but by His guidance. He holds the key; He *is* the key. Revealed truth can be known only through the Revealer. Ignoring this, scholars and historians, grammarians and antiquarians, critics and agnostics, are blind in the midst of light. The same result is seen in the belief about our Lord Jesus Christ, the experience of grace, and the doctrine of the Church. No man can say Jesus is Lord save by the Holy Ghost, but men are seeking to interpret the Christ in terms of reason, history, and philosophy. The Christian religion, however, begins in a new birth in the power of the Spirit. It is developed under His guidance and sustained by His presence; but ignoring the Spirit, it becomes a matter of education and evolution. The Church is the Body of Christ begotten, unified, and indwelt by the Spirit; but, forgetting the Spirit, men wrangle over limbs, functions, and orders. The Christian religion is hopeless without the Holy Ghost.

The Problems of the Church

As in truth, so it is in service. The Church is helpless without the presence and power of the Spirit. The Church has never talked so much about itself and its problems. That is always a bad sign. The lust for talk about work increases as the power for work declines. Conferences multiply when work fails. The problems of the Church are never solved by talking about them. The problems arise out of failures. There is no need to discuss the problem of reaching the masses as long as the masses are being reached. There is no problem of empty churches as long as churches are full. There is no class-meeting question as long as the class-meeting throbs with life and ministers to the manifold needs of heart and life. The power to attract is in attractiveness, and it is useless to advertise the banquet if there is nothing to eat. We, however, are acting as though the only remedy for decline were method, organization, and compromise. The Church is failing to meet modern needs, grip the modern mind, and save modern life. The saints are the ordained rulers of the earth, but they do not rule; indeed, they have dropped the scepter and repudiated the responsibility.

The helplessness of the Church is pathetic and tragic. There might be no such Person as the Holy Ghost.

Believers Without the Holy Ghost

The Church knows quite well both the reason and the remedy for failure. The human resources of the Church were never so great. The opportunities of the Church were never so glorious. The need for the work of the Church was never so urgent. The crisis is momentous; and the Church staggers helplessly amid it all. When the ancient Church reproached God with sleeping at the post of duty, God charged His people with being staggering drunk. The Church knows perfectly well what is the matter. It is sheer cant to seek the explanation in changed conditions. When were conditions ever anything else? The Church has lost the note of authority, the secret of wisdom, and the gift of power through its persistent and willful neglect of the Holy Spirit of God. Confusion and impotence are inevitable when the wisdom and resources of the world are substituted for the presence and power of the Spirit of God.

Proofs abound. The New Testament furnishes examples of churches filled with the Spirit and churches without the Spirit. The differences are obvious. The church in Ephesus of which Apollos was minister had not so much as heard that the Spirit was given. The churches in our day have no such excuse. Ours is the sin of denial. He has been shut out from the province in which He is indispensable. Religion has been reconstructed without Him. There is no denial of the supernatural, but it is insisted that the supernatural must conform to natural law. It is admitted that truth is inspired, but its inspiration must develop along the lines of natural selection and growth. Religion cannot be allowed to have come upon any other lines than those of literature, philosophy, and ethics. The Christian religion has simply the honor of being less faulty than the rest. Jesus Christ must be accounted for in the same way. He is simply the crown and consummation of a progressive humanity. The emphasis is upon the Man, and in that emphasis there is reason to rejoice, but the strange thing is that in the intense interest in Jesus the certainties about Him that come through the Spirit have been lost.

Doctrine Without Experience

The Church still has a theology of the Holy Ghost but it has no living consciousness of His presence and power. Theology without experience is like faith without works: it is dead. The signs of death abound. Prayer meetings have died out because men did not believe in the Holy Ghost. The liberty of prophesying has gone because men believe in investigation and not in inspiration. There is a dearth of conversions because faith about the new birth as a creative act of the Holy Ghost has lost its grip on intellect and heart. The experience of the Second Gift of Grace is no longer preached and testified, because Christian experience, though it may have to begin in the Spirit, must be perfected in the wisdom of the flesh and the culture of the schools. Confusion and impotence are the inevitable results when the wisdom and resources of the world are substituted for the presence and power of the Spirit.

The rebound from materialism is seen in such recent movements as Christian Science, Spiritualism, and Theosophy. It is the truth in these things that gives them their power, and it is useless to denounce them. They are the reaction of the spirit of man against the bondage of the flesh and of the mind. The cravings they represent must be met by the experience of Pentecost. Modernism and mysticism are also the products of a religion that is not baptized of the Holy Ghost. Sacerdotalism is another. These things flourish on impoverished soil and dunghills. They are the works of the flesh and the product of spiritual death. The remedy for them is not in reproach and bitterness, but in floods and rivers, winds and sun—the energizing of the Spirit. The answer is in the demonstration of a supernatural religion, and the only way to a supernatural religion is in the abiding presence of the Spirit of God.

2

The Church
Without the Spirit

THE CHURCH is the creation of the Holy Spirit. It is a community of believers who owe their religious life from first to last to the Spirit. Apart from Him there can be neither Christian nor Church. The Christian religion is not institutional but experiential. It is not by an ordained class, neither is it in ordinances and sacraments. It is not a fellowship of common interest in culture, virtue or service. Membership is by spiritual birth. The roll of membership is kept in heaven. Christ is the Door. He knows those who are His, and they know Him. The church roll and the Lamb's Book of Life are not always identical. "No man can say, Jesus is Lord, but in the Holy Spirit," and confession of the lordship of Jesus Christ is the first condition of membership in His Church. The command to tarry in the city until there came the enduement of power from on high proves that the one essential equipment of the Church is the gift of the Holy Ghost. Nothing else avails for the real work of the Church. For much that is undertaken by churches today He is not necessary. The Holy Ghost is no more needed to run bazaars, social clubs, institutions and picnics than He is to run a circus. These may be necessary adjuncts of a modern church, but it is not for power to run these things that we have need to tarry. Religious services and organized institutions do not constitute a Christian church, and these may flourish without the gift of Pentecostal fire.

The Life of the Body

The work of the Spirit in the Church is set forth in the promises of Jesus on the eve of His departure and demonstrated in the Acts of the Apostles. The Gospels tell of "all that Jesus began to do and to teach, until the day in which He was received up," and the Acts of the Apostles tell of all that He continued to do and to teach *after* the day in which He was received up. The Holy Spirit is the active, administrative Agent of the glorified Son. He is the Paraclete, the Deputy, the acting Representative of the ascended Christ. His mission is to glorify Christ by perpetuating His character, establishing His Kingdom, and accomplishing His redeeming purpose in the world. The Church is the Body of Christ, and the Spirit is the Spirit of Christ. He fills the Body, directs its movements, controls its members, inspires its wisdom, supplies its strength. He guides into the truth, sanctifies its agents, and empowers for witnessing. The work of the Church is to "minister the Spirit," to speak His message and transmit His power. He calls and distributes, controls and guides, inspires and strengthens.

The Spirit has never abdicated His authority nor relegated His power. Neither Pope nor Parliament, neither Conference nor Council is supreme in the Church of Christ. Any church that is man-managed instead of God-governed is doomed to failure. A ministry that is college-trained but not Spirit-filled works no miracles. The church that multiplies committees and neglects prayer may be fussy, noisy, enterprising, but it labors in vain and spends its strength for naught. It is possible to excel in mechanics and fail in dynamic. There is a superabundance of machinery; what is wanting is power. To run an organization needs no God. Man can supply the energy, enterprise and enthusiasm for things human. The real work of a church depends upon the power of the Spirit.

The presence of the Spirit is vital and central to the work of the Church. Nothing else avails. Apart from Him wisdom becomes folly, and strength weakness. The Church is called to be a "spiritual house" and a holy priesthood. Only spiritual people can be its "living stones," and only the Spirit-filled its priests. Scholarship is blind to spiritual truth till He reveals. Worship is idolatry till He inspires. Preaching is powerless if it be not a demonstration of His power. Prayer is vain unless He energizes. Human resources of learning and organization, wealth and enthusiasm, reform and philanthropy, are worse than useless if there be no Holy Ghost in them. The Church always fails at the point of self-confidence. When a church is run on the same lines as a circus, there may be crowds, but there is no Shekinah. That is why prayer is the test of faith and the secret of power. The Spirit of God travails in the prayer-life of the soul. Miracles are the direct work of His power, and without miracle the church cannot live. The carnal can argue, but it is the Spirit that convicts. Education can civilize, but it is being born of the Spirit that saves. The energy of the flesh can run bazaars, organize amusements, and raise millions; but it is the presence of the Holy Spirit that makes a temple of the Living God. The root trouble of the current distress is that the Church has more faith in the world and the flesh than in the Holy Ghost, and things will get no better till we get back to His realized presence and power. The breath of the four winds would turn death into life and dry bones into mighty armies, but it only comes by prayer.

Form and Spirit

The Acts of the Apostles gives us an account of a nascent church destitute of the Spirit. The picture corresponds in many particulars with that of the church in the Apocalypse that had lost its Christ. The church in Laodicea was rich and respectable, prosperous and influential, complacent and confident, but was blind to the tragedy on the doorstep. Their worship was faultless in form and passionless in spirit. There was no heresy in their creed, but there was no fire in their souls. The Spirit of Christ was outside. Ephesus and Laodicea have much in common, for where Christ is dishonored there can be no Pentecost.

The newly-born church at Ephesus had the advantage of a distinguished and brilliant preacher. He was a man of great scholarship, who had won distinction at a great university. No preacher can have too much learning, and the Bible gives due recognition to the fact that Apollos was "a learned man." In addition to the wisdom of the schools, "he was mighty in the Scriptures." Some preachers have finished their ministerial training with the confession that they had learned less about their Bibles than about any other subject; but this man had been taught the Scriptures and "instructed in the way of the Lord." His teaching was Scriptural, orthodox, careful. To scholarship he added passion. This accomplished scholar, Scriptural in doctrine and careful in exegesis, literally "boiled over in spirit." Enthusiasm does not often accompany scholarship; it is bad form among cultured people. Religious fervor generally declines with the advance of education. Much learning has a tendency to make cold, dry preachers. This was a rare type of college-made preacher. His fervor survived success in study and he came through his course intense and scholarly, fervent and accurate, faithful and accomplished, courageous and cultured.

It seems hardly credible that such a minister should lack the very things essential for the work of the Christian ministry. He had neither complete gospel nor full power. In his preaching there was no personal cross, no personal resurrection, no personal Pentecost. He preached Jesus, but he did not know Christ crucified. Peter the fisherman was worth a thousand of him. Eloquent, learned, Scriptural, impassioned, faithful and courageous, Apollos had an incomplete gospel. Carefully trained, well-instructed, a courageous learner and an effective teacher, he had but partial vision. Skilled in definition, powerful in debate, earnest in advocacy, he had no real power. The colleges had given him of their best, but they had left him ignorant of things vital and destitute of the Holy Ghost.

Like priest, like people. Like minister, like members. Truth comes through personality; and the level of a preacher's experience determines both the range and level of the sermon. It also determines the level to which he can help others. John's baptism in the pulpit resulted in a corresponding religion in the pew. It was a cold-water gospel and a cold-water piety. To Paul's keen eye there was something wanting. They were sternly devout, orderly, reverent; but it was not Christian worship and experience. Their heads were bowed and their faces gave evidence of discipline, but they were not radiant. Their lives were marked by strict integrity, for John's cold-water religion was severely moral. They were as fervent as they were upright, and as religious as they were conscientious. Their religion was marked by a spirit of deep penitence and godly fear. They were upright in life, fervent in religion, devout in spirit, faithful in service; and yet, without the Holy Ghost. Their religion was a strict, external observance; not an indwelling Presence. They lived by rule, not by illumination. God saves from within; they disciplined themselves from without. Religion to them was a joyless burden, for they carried their God on their backs instead of in their hearts.

The Difference Holy Ghost Fire Makes

Pentecost transforms the preacher. The commonest bush ablaze with the presence of God becomes a miracle of glory. Under its influence the feeble become as David, and the choice mighty "as the angel of the Lord." The ministry energized by the Holy Ghost is marked by aggressive evangelism, social revolution, and persecution. Holy Ghost preaching led to the burning of the books of the magic art, and it stirred up the opposition of those who trafficked in the ruin of the people. Indifference to religion is impossible where the preacher is a flame of fire. To the church, Pentecost brought light, power, joy. There came to each illumination of mind, assurance of heart, intensity of love, fullness of power, exuberance of joy. No one needed to ask if they had received the Holy Ghost. Fire is self-evident. So is power! Even demons know the difference between the power of inspiration and the correctness of instruction. Secondhand gospels work no miracles. Uninspired devices end in defeat and shame. The only power that is adequate for Christian life and Christian work is the power of the Holy Ghost.

The work of God is not by might of man or by the power of men, but by His Spirit. It is by Him the truth convicts and converts, sanctifies and saves. The philosophies of men fail, but the Word of God in the demonstration of the Spirit prevails. Our wants are many and our faults innumerable, but they are all comprehended in our lack of the Holy Ghost. We need nothing but the fire.

The resources of the Church are in "the supply of the Spirit." The Spirit is more than merely the minister of consolation, the "Comforter." He is Christ without the limitations of the flesh and the material world. He can reveal what Christ could not speak. He has resources of power greater than those Christ could use, and He makes possible greater works than His. He is the Spirit of God, the Spirit of Truth, the Spirit of Witness, the Spirit of Conviction, the Spirit of Power, the Spirit of Holiness, the Spirit of Life, the Spirit of Adoption, the Spirit of Help, the Spirit of Liberty, the Spirit of Wisdom, the Spirit of Revelation, the Spirit of Promise, the Spirit of Love, the Spirit of Meekness, the Spirit of Sound Mind, the Spirit of Grace, the Spirit of Glory, and the Spirit of Prophecy. It is for the Church to explore the resources of the Spirit. The resources of the world are futile. The resources of the Church within herself are inadequate. In the fullness of the Spirit there is abundance of wisdom, resources, and power; but a man-managed, world-annexing, priest-pretending Church can never save the world or fulfill the mission of Christ.

Suppose we try Pentecost!

3

"The Spirit of Promise"

THE DIVINE Spirit is called "the Holy Spirit of Promise." The expression looks both backward and forward. He is the Spirit given in fulfillment of promise, and in Him is the earnest of the promise as yet unfulfilled. The gift of Pentecost fulfills the crowning promise of the Father. The Spirit is the Promised One. Our Lord spoke of Him as "the promise of the Father," and on the day of Pentecost the Apostle Peter, in explanation of the descent of the Holy Spirit, declared: "This Jesus did God raise up, whereof we all are witnesses. Being therefore by the right hand of God exalted, and having received of the Father the promise of the Holy Ghost, He hath poured forth this, which we see and hear." Pentecost was God's seal upon the Messiahship of Jesus and the fulfilling of His promise to Israel. Fulfillment brings new promises. Attainment inspires new hopes. The Spirit comes to the believing disciples as the earnest of inheritance through sonship and the pledge of our resurrection in Christ the risen Lord and Saviour. He is the Spirit of Promise in fulfillment, and the Spirit of Promise in assurance through faith.

The Promise of the Father

Throughout the development of the Old Testament revelation the promise of the Spirit is always closely identified with the person and ministry of the Messiah. In the earlier stages He is conceived as a power rather than as a Person, but in Him is always revealed a Person who is an active Agent, and not a mere influence emanating from God. There was little knowledge of Him as a distinct Person with whom man could hold personal intercourse, but in slow stages there emerged a Living Person in whom was the fullness of divine wisdom and power. In Him was the secret of the redemptive and sovereign power of the servant of the Lord who would save Israel, and through Israel redeem the world.

Our Lord claimed that these promises concerning the Spirit were to be fulfilled in Him. John the Baptist baptized with water, but the Christ came to baptize with the Holy Ghost and with fire. He claimed the fulfillment of prophecy in the gift of the Spirit to Him in Jordan, and He claimed it also in the gift of the Spirit to the world. There are few incidents more illuminating than that recorded of "the last day of the Feast," in John 7:37–39. The Feast was the Feast of Tabernacles. The festival proper lasted seven days, during which all Israel dwelt in booths. Special sacrifices were offered and special rites observed. Every morning one of the priests brought water from the pool of Siloam, and amidst the sounding of trumpets and other demonstrations of joy the water was poured upon the altar. The rite was a celebration and a prophecy.

It commemorated the miraculous supply of water in the wilderness, and it bore witness to the expectation of the coming of the Spirit. On the seventh day the ceremony of the poured water ceased, but the eighth day was a day of holy convocation, the greatest day of all. On that day there was *no* water poured upon the altar, and it was on the waterless day that Jesus stood on the spot and cried, saying: "If any man thirst, let him come unto Me and drink." Then He added these words: "He that believeth on Me, as the Scripture hath said, from within him shall flow rivers of living water." The Apostle adds the interpretive comment: "But this spake He of the Spirit, which they that believe on Him were to receive: for the Spirit was not yet given; because Jesus was not yet glorified."

"As the Scripture hath said." There is no such passage in the Scripture as that quoted, but the prophetic part of the water ceremony was based upon certain Old Testament symbols and prophecies in which water flowed forth from Zion to cleanse, renew, and fructify the world. A study of Joel 3:18 and Ezekiel 47 will supply the key to the meaning, both of the rite and our Lord's promise. The Holy Ghost was "not yet given" but He was promised, and His coming would be from the place of blood, the altar of sacrifice. Calvary opened the fountain from which was poured forth the blessing of Pentecost. The descent of the Spirit depended upon the ascent of the Son.

The Promise of the Son

The promise of the Father becomes explicit in the

promise of Jesus.

For the greater part of His ministry He rarely mentioned the Spirit. On the eve of His Passion He spoke of Him with amazing fullness. Until then there had been no need to speak of Him, except to warn those who were in danger of "eternal sin" through their blasphemy against the Holy Ghost. Neither were they ready to hear of Him. When the time came for the Son to return to the Father, it was necessary that His own should know about the Comforter whom He would send to them. The promise is complete. It summed up all the teaching of prophecy and anticipated all the development in experience. Those who would know the doctrine and work of the Spirit should study carefully the words spoken about Him in the Upper Room. They should be underlined, searched into, read over and over again, and prayed through till they are received into the mind and made the possession of the heart. There are seven fundamental statements about the Spirit in the promise of the Son.

(1) That the self-same Spirit that had been given to the Son would be given to them.

(2) That He would be to them all that He had been to Him.

(3) That He would be to them all that the Son had been to them and more.

(4) That He would be *in* them as the Son had been *with* them.

(5) That they would gain in Him more than they would lose in the departure of Christ.

(6) That He would be the Paraclete, or Other Self

of the Christ, and through His indwelling the Christ would live in them.

(7) That His mission was to glorify the Son by taking of the things of Christ and making them available to us.

Jesus called the Holy Spirit the Paraclete. It is unfortunate that "Paraclete" should have been translated "Comforter," for the ministry of consolation hardly enters into Christ's promise. The margin of the Revised Version suggests the Latin word "Advocate" as the nearest equivalent to Paraclete, and if "Advocate" is substituted for "Comforter" in John 14 to 16 it is astonishing how illuminating it becomes. The Spirit is not *our* Advocate, but *Christ's*. An advocate appears as representative of another, and the Holy Spirit comes to represent Christ, interpret and vindicate Christ, administer for Christ in His Church and Kingdom; to be to the believer all that Christ Himself was and is—with this difference: that the Christ was *with* His disciples and the Spirit is *in* them.

The Promise of the Spirit

St. Paul speaks of "the supply of the Spirit." All the promises of God are made possible by the Holy Spirit. All our needs are met in His supply. He is the all-inclusive gift. In Him, and by Him, and through Him is the supply of all our need. He is the Spirit of Truth and Life, of wisdom and might, of grace and love. He knows the deep things of God and teaches the heart the secret of prayer. He takes of the things of Christ and makes them known to both mind and heart.

He is the source of divine energy and power, and through Him the inner man receives strength. "The supply of the Spirit" fulfills every need.

The Church is delegated as the minister of this supply. The measure of our usefulness is the measure of the supply of the Spirit which we bring. The work of God is not by might, nor by power, but by the Spirit of the living God. It is useless to attempt in the energy of the flesh what can be accomplished only in the power of the Holy Ghost. The promise of the Spirit covers every present need and guarantees the consummation of redeeming grace. He is both seal and earnest. He secures us to God for an inheritance for His own possession; and He secures to us a glorious, complete, and eternal inheritance in God. That is why the gift of the Spirit always sets the heart singing. Its confidence is unwavering, its power is invincible, and its joy unspeakable.

Have ye received the Holy Ghost? There are many who have believed of whom the words of John are still true: He is "not yet given," and the reason is the same, for the coronation gift always comes when the King is crowned.

4

Pentecost

WHAT happened at Pentecost? There was something that began a new era for the world, a new power of righteousness, a new mission of redemption, and a new basis of fellowship. What was it that made Pentecost the birthday of the Church of Christ? It is not enough to say the Holy Spirit was given. In what sense was He given?

Before Pentecost

The Spirit of God has been active in the world from the beginning. He brooded upon the face of the waters when the earth was without form and void, and the order of creation was the result of His brooding. In the Old Testament He is the creative Agent, Sustainer, and Renewer of the world of nature. He is the Lord and Giver of life. In Ezekiel's vision the forces and machinery of nature were impelled and controlled by the Spirit of God that dwelt in the wheels. It was God's gift of His Spirit to man in creation that distinguished man from the rest of His works. What

else can it mean when it is said, "And the Lord God
formed man of the dust of the ground, and breathed
into his nostrils the breath of life; and man became a
living soul"? Breath is the word for Spirit. It is a picture
word. God does not breathe. The Spirit is not wind. It
is a figure of speech to illustrate the fact that God
communicated to man the life which was within
Himself. God breathed into man His Spirit, and man
became a living being. It was by the Spirit of God that
man was made in the image of God, and it was by the
breath of God in His Son that there was given unto
man again the gift of the Holy Ghost. On the evening
of Easter Day the risen Lord breathed upon His
disciples and said, "Receive ye the Holy Ghost." He
communicated to them the Life which He had in
Himself. "There is a spirit in man, and the breath of
the Almighty giveth understanding." "The Spirit of
God hath made me, and the breath of the Almighty
giveth me life." All through the Old Testament the
Holy Spirit is creative, directive, energizing. He came
upon Moses, Bezaleel, Samson, Gideon, Samuel; and
all the prophets spoke by Him. Every creative period
had its gift of the Holy Ghost. The manifestations are
occasional and special. There is in them a consciousness of limitation and incompleteness, and
prophets like Isaiah and Joel foretold a day of fullness
of the Spirit which would be the crowning gift of
redeeming grace. In the New Testament the Spirit of
God is the active Agent in salvation, but in the Gospels
He was "not yet given," and our Lord Himself was
straitened until His baptism was accomplished and He
had "sent fire upon the earth." The Spirit was in the

world, but "not yet given."

At Pentecost

At Pentecost the Holy Spirit came as He had never come before. The signs were not new except in their combination and intensity. The wind and the fire and the tongues had all been associated with the gift of the Spirit, but they were now intensified, enlarged, and distributed to a community of believers. There was a sense of overflowing fullness. Something had happened in the cosmic order that sent forth the Spirit of God in larger measure, with new powers and enlarged opportunities. He was the gift of God to His Son, and the gift of His Son to the world. He came to fulfill the mission for which Christ came into the world. He is our Lord's Paraclete, His Advocate and Administrator. His ministry is redemptive and regenerative. In Him the risen and ascended Lord finds His enlarged opportunity. The straitening is past. He is exalted far above all rule, and authority, and dominion, and power, and to Him are given all authority in heaven and on earth, and the fullness of "Him that filleth all in all."

Christ had said, "It is better for you that I go away, for if I go not away, the Comforter, the Paraclete, will not come to you." The inference is that the presence of the Spirit is better than the bodily presence of Jesus. That is a strange word. Why could not the Spirit come if Jesus did not go away? Why should the coming of the Spirit wait for the going of Jesus? It is not difficult to understand that the Spirit found the fullest opportunity of manifestation in Jesus; to none but Jesus had He ever been able to come "without measure." But why wait to come upon such men as Peter and James and John?

The gift of the Spirit is inseparable from the work of the Son. Is it not true to say that Deity gained new experience of humanity in Jesus Christ? Our Great High Priest learned obedience by the things He suffered, and because He is touched with the feeling of our infirmities He is able to succor and mighty to save. By the sufferings of Christ the Throne of God is the Throne of Grace where mercy and help are found. If Jesus needed to learn that He might be our Great High Priest, was there not a reason for waiting till that was accomplished before the Spirit could be given? The Scriptures are reticent about the Holy Spirit, which means that the Spirit is reticent about Himself, but they do make it clear that the Spirit is the crowning gift of redemption through Jesus Christ, and the Spirit was through it all. As the Son learned and thereby entered into the Priesthood of Grace, so the Spirit was prepared to be His Paraclete in the Church and the world. In the fullness of time God sent forth His Son, and when the Day of Pentecost was fully come, "they were all together in one place. And suddenly there came from heaven a sound as of the rushing of a mighty wind, and it filled all the house where they were sitting. And there appeared unto them tongues parting asunder, like as of fire; and it sat upon each one of them. And they were all filled with the Holy Spirit, and began to speak with other tongues, as the Spirit gave them utterance."

After Pentecost

The change in the Apostles was more wonderful than any of the marvelous portents of the day. The wind and the fire passed, but the transformation remained. It was easy to see the difference in Peter, but it was no greater in him than in the rest. All that Jesus had promised had come to pass. Pentecost interprets the Upper Room. The Paraclete had come, and they were comforted. The Spirit of Truth had come, and they knew. The witness to the Christ had come, and they became witnesses. The Executant of the Kingdom had come in power, and each found himself under authority and speaking as the Spirit gave him utterance. Fear had gone. They no longer sat with closed windows and bolted doors for fear of the Jews. They feared no one. They were afraid of nothing. They no longer spoke with bated breath. They proclaimed the truth concerning Jesus in the open streets of the city where Jesus had been murdered, and within six weeks of His death. A new power was at work. The Lord Jesus had said that when the Spirit was come He would convict of sin, and righteousness, and judgment; and, lo, multitudes were smitten, and three thousand souls cried for mercy. It was indeed "a great and notable day." The world had never seen such a day. The angels had never seen such a day. Neither had Satan and his hosts of spiritual darkness ever seen such a day.

The vital thing that happened at Pentecost is that the Spirit of Jesus came to abide in the hearts of men in the power of God. That is the difference Pentecost made. "Ye know Him, for He abideth with you and shall be in you." It is the difference from *with* to *in,* plus the difference in Christ by His exaltation and coronation. Through that indwelling Presence Pentecost makes us one with Christ as the Son is one with the Father: "I in you, and ye in Me." So the Spirit brings the Life of Jesus into the soul; by Him we say, "Christ liveth in me."

What did Pentecost do for men? It brought a new dynamic of righteousness. From the beginning there has been the light lighting every man that cometh into the world; a light the darkness could neither apprehend nor overcome. In the incarnation of the Word made flesh the Light came into the world. Pentecost focused the Light. He convicts the world of sin, of righteousness, and of judgment. There is a new power of conviction. Men were pricked in their hearts as they had never been pricked before. That conviction centers in Christ and is wrought by the Spirit.

Pentecost brought a new fellowship. That is the abiding miracle. Community of the Spirit of Jesus issued in community of life in His name. The Kingdom of God henceforth is a new theocracy, permeated, dominated, sanctified in the Spirit of Pentecost. The new thing is not in the wind and fire, or the gift of tongues, but in the possession of the Spirit by each for the good of all.

That which happened at Pentecost is the biggest thing that ever happened. And now the biggest question of all is, has it happened to you and me? Have ye received the Holy Ghost?

5

The Gift of the Holy Ghost

PENTECOST is the crowning miracle and abiding mystery of grace. It marks the beginning of the Christian dispensation. The tongues of fire sat upon each one of them. The word "sat" in Scripture marks an end and a beginning. The process of preparation is ended, and the established order has begun. It marks the end of creation and the beginning of normal forces. "In six days the Lord made heaven and earth, the sea, and all that in them is, and rested the seventh day." There was no weariness in God. He did not rest from fatigue. What it means is that all creative work was accomplished. The same figure of speech is used of the Redeemer. Of Him it is said: "When He had made purification of sins, [He] sat down on the right hand of the Majesty on high." No other priest had sat down. The priests of the Temple ministered standing, because their ministry was provisional and preparatory, a parable and a prophecy. Christ's own ministry was part of the preparation for the coming of the Spirit. Until He "sat down" in glory, there could be no dispensation of the Spirit. John says of our Lord's promise in the Temple: "This spake He of the Spirit, which they that believed on Him were to receive: for the Spirit was not yet given; because Jesus was not yet glorified." The descent of the One waited for the ascent of the Other. When the work of redemption was complete the Spirit was given, and when He came He "sat." He reigns in the Church, as Christ reigns in the heavenly realms. This is the dispensation of the Spirit.

The Holy Ghost is God's gift to the Church of His Son. For the work of redemption the Son of God emptied Himself of the prerogatives of His divine status, but for His ministry the Father gave Him the Spirit, and at its close "He made Him to sit at His right hand in the heavenly sphere, far above all rule, and authority, and power, and dominion, and every name that is named, not only in this world, but also in that which is to come: and He put all things in subjection under His feet, and gave Him to be head over all things to the Church which is His Body, the fullness of Him that filleth all in all." Pentecost is the sequel of the Son's investiture. "Being therefore by the right hand of God exalted, and having received of the Father the promise of the Holy Ghost, He hath poured forth this, which ye see and hear."

The Spirit in the Church

The sphere of the Spirit is in the living temple of sanctified humanity. He dwells not in temples made with hands. The Temple at Jerusalem was a permitted mistake, as surely as the kingship of Israel. In the New Jerusalem there is no Temple. The Tabernacle was a type of heavenly realities. The Temple sought to give solidity, permanence, and magnificence to that which God meant to be provisional and typical. God cares nothing for costly buildings and everything for loving hearts. He seeks men. He wants men. He needs men. He dwells in men. Immanuel is the first word and the last of the gospel of grace. In a powerful plea for the life of prayer, E. M. Bounds says: "God's plan is to make much of the man, far more of him than of anything else. Men are God's method. The Church is looking for better methods; God is looking for better men." He has staked His Kingdom on men. He has trusted His gospel to men. He has given His Spirit to men. The Church is on the stretch for new methods, new plans, new buildings, new organizations, but "the eyes of the Lord run to and fro throughout the earth, to show Himself strong in the behalf of them whose heart is perfect towards Him." The Holy Ghost does not come upon methods, but upon men. He does not anoint machinery, but men. He does not work through organizations, but through men. He does not dwell in buildings, but in men. He indwells the Body of Christ, directs its activities, distributes its forces, empowers its members.

Those gathered in that Upper Room "when the Day of Pentecost was fully come" had been prepared for His coming. They were disciples who acknowledged the Lordship of Jesus. They had realized His saving power and surrendered all to His sovereign will. For ten days they had been in prayer, and for the greater part of three years they had sat at the feet of

Jesus. When they realized His Sonship He blessed them, and now the promise of the fiery baptism is fulfilled. The Spirit "sat upon each one of them; and they were all filled with the Holy Ghost." He had come to reign over each and all. Jesus Christ had defined His mission and outlined His program. He was to unify them into one Body, guide them into all truth, and strengthen them for all service. In the Church He is the supreme executive, but He has His seat in the soul. He directs all things from the spiritual center of the inner life. The body prepared for the eternal Son was born of a Virgin; the body prepared for the indwelling Spirit is begotten of faith in Jesus Christ, the Son of the living God. The Church is the sphere of His ministry, the agent of His purpose, the place of His Presence.

The Spirit in the Believer

"The Spirit sat upon each one of them. And they were all filled." The whole is for each, and each is for all. The story of Pentecost reveals what the gift did for individual men as well as for the whole company. Peter moves in the blaze of the sun. Throughout the Gospel narrative he is a man of generous impulses, with many failings. He utters his resolves with the emphasis of the irresolute, and often fails in the hour of testing. Pentecost reveals him transformed. He has the certainty of revealed truth in his speech, and the confidence of invincible power in his bearing. The man who cringed and sulked a few days ago stands upon both feet, utterly destitute of fear. Temperament and natural aptitude are unchanged, but the man is radiant with a new energy, transfigured with a new Spirit, effective with a new power. The Spirit of Christ has clothed Himself with Peter. He speaks with the same Galilean accent; but the utterance is of the Holy Ghost. St. Paul put the same truth another way when he said: "I have been crucified with Christ; yet I live; and yet no longer I, but Christ liveth in me." The indwelling Presence is clothed with sanctified manhood and becomes the very life of life, and the very soul of the soul. "I live; yet no longer I."

The Apostle attributes all spiritual effectiveness to the indwelling power. "Our sufficiency," he says, "is of God who also hath made us able ministers of the New Testament, not of the letter, but of the spirit; for the letter killeth, but the spirit giveth life." There are other kinds of ability than that which comes of God through the Spirit, but they are death-dealing and never life-giving. It is the Spirit that quickens. Everything else fails. The letter may be faultlessly orthodox, the method may be marvelously ingenious, the man may be tremendously earnest, but only the God-made, God-inspired, God-enabled avails. Carnalities kill. The power that quickens, transforms, perfects, is of God the Spirit. There never was so much human perfection in the Church, but the New Jerusalem is not built up by the powers of Babylon; it comes down out of heaven from God. Believers without the Holy Ghost cannot do the work of the Spirit.

The Spirit in the World

It is this mystery that has filled the history of the Church with anomalies. Inadequate men are always doing impossible things, and ordinary men achieve extraordinary results. God's biggest things seem to be done by the most unlikely people. Unknown Davids kill terrifying Goliaths. The weak confound the mighty, and things hid from the learned and wise are made known to unlearned and ignorant men. The All-wise seems to delight in nothing so much as turning the wisdom of the vain to folly, and the strength of the proud to shame. He has declared the insufficiency of all but Himself, but man struts and sets himself to demonstrate his own sufficiency. Pride of logic, pride of skill, pride of personality, pride of power, perpetuate the spirit of Babel in the Church of God with the same inevitable result. It ends in defeat, disaster, and dishonor. There is no conquest of the world for God but by the Holy Ghost. He alone can convict the world "in respect of sin, and of righteousness, and of judgment." There is no other power that can do that, and without conviction there can be neither the salvation of the soul nor the coming of the Kingdom. Our one lack is the power that comes of the Spirit. For holiness and for service, for prosperity and for victory, He is our one need. The Spirit is God's gift. The power cannot be bought either with money or merit. A gift can only be received or rejected. This gift is for all who believe and crown Jesus Christ in their hearts.

6

The Pentecostal Life

WHEN Andrew Murray was led to write on "The Temple of the Holy Spirit," he said with reverential awe: "I will meditate and be still, until something of the overwhelming glory of the truth fall upon me, and faith begin to realize it: I am His temple, and in the secret place He sits upon the throne." Then, when he had written, this prayer rises like incense: "I do now tremblingly accept the blessed truth: God the Spirit, the Holy Spirit who is God Almighty, dwells in me. O, my Father, reveal within me what it means, lest I sin against Thee by saying it and not living it."

Hour after hour, since I wrote the headlines of this chapter, my mind has been held in the same reverential awe. I have written and preached much on the Holy Spirit, for the knowledge of Him has been the most vital fact of my experience. I owe everything to the gift of Pentecost. It came to me when I was not seeking it. I was about my heavenly Father's business, seeking means whereby I could do the work to which He had called and sent me, and in my search I came across a prophet, heard a testimony, and set out to seek I knew not what. I knew that it was a bigger thing than I had ever known. It came along the line of duty, in a crisis of obedience. When it came I could not explain what had happened, but I was aware of things unspeakable and full of glory. Some results were immediate. There came into my soul a deep peace, a thrilling joy, and a new sense of power. My mind was quickened. Every power was vitalized. My bodily powers were quickened. There was a new sense of spring and vitality, a new power of endurance, and a strong man's exhilaration in big things. Things began to happen. What we had failed to do by strenuous endeavor came to pass without labor. It was as when the Lord Jesus stepped into the boat that with all their rowing had made no progress, "immediately the ship was at the land whither they went." It was gloriously wonderful.

The things that happened were the least part of the experience. The wind and the fire and the tongues excited most comment, but they vanished, and it was the realities that remained that were most wonderful. The experience gave me the key to all my thinking, all my service, and all my life. Pentecost gave me the key to the Scriptures. It has kept my feet in all the slippery places of all sorts of criticism. The things that are stumbling blocks to so many are stepping stones to me. The inexplicable becomes plain when we recognize the presence and law of the Spirit. It balances scholarship, and gives discernment beyond all human learning. Indeed, learning without the Holy Ghost blinds men to the realities of divine truth. The man who thinks he can know the Word of God by mere intellectual study is greatly deceived. Spiritual truth is spiritually discerned. The soul sees with the eyes of the heart, and they are opened by the Holy Spirit. The knowledge He gives is something more than information: it is knowledge that leads to trust, knowledge that brings life, and knowledge that inspires love. The same Spirit gave me a new understanding and experience of prayer, and with these gifts there came a new enduement of wisdom and power. From the first day of my Pentecost I became a seeker and a winner of souls.

A Definite Experience

The Baptism of the Holy Spirit is a definite and distinct experience assured and verified by the witness of the Spirit. The disciples who were commanded to tarry until they were "endued with power from on high" had already received the Spirit for salvation. It is puerile to say they were not already saved. Our Lord places that question forever beyond doubt in His intercession for them on the eve of His Passion. They were his. He had kept them by His power, given them His cleansing word, and they were not of the world even as He was not of the world. Still, they were commanded to tarry for the fullness of the Spirit. Of the believers at Samaria it was said that when Peter and John came down they prayed for them that they might receive the Holy Ghost, for as yet He was fallen upon none of them despite their baptism in the name of the Lord Jesus (Acts 8:14–17). Of the group of believers at Ephesus, Paul asked: "Have ye received the Holy Ghost since ye believed?" The Revised Version renders it, "Did ye receive the Holy Ghost when ye believed?" (Acts 19:2). Whichever the case, the receiving of the Holy Ghost was so definite an experience that they were expected to know whether they had received the gift or not. Their answer was an emphatic "No," and they added that they had not so much as heard whether the Holy Ghost was given.

The experience is distinct from that of regeneration. Of those Samaritans who had believed and been baptized in the name of the Lord Jesus it was said they had not yet been baptized of the Holy Ghost. It is evident, therefore, that a man may be born again of the Spirit and not be baptized with the Spirit. In regeneration there is a gift of life by the Spirit, and whosoever receives it is saved; in the Baptism of the Spirit there is a gift of power, and by it the believer is equipped for service and endued for witnessing. In the Corinthian Church there were many believers who were not filled with the Holy Ghost, though they were rich in the gifts of the Spirit. Nevertheless, it is the inheritance of every believer to receive the gift of the Spirit, to be baptized with the Spirit, to be filled with the Spirit; and to this definite experience thousands have testified. They were born again of the Spirit, and afterwards—sometimes a long time after, and sometimes after a little while—there came a conviction of need and an assurance of faith through the Word of God by which they entered into an experience of sanctification and the abiding fullness of the Spirit.

The question of Paul to the converts of Apollos implies that it is possible to be filled with the Spirit at conversion, but it clearly proves that we may be Christians and *not* filled with the Spirit. There are many Christians of whose devotion and Christian experience there can be no doubt who have never had a Pentecost; and they know it. Sometimes they grieve over their lack and sigh for the blessing, but it is possible to be saved and go to heaven without ever having known the Pentecostal fullness of the indwelling Presence. Pentecost is the gift of power. The Spirit fills, vitalizes, and energizes with the power of God. Deliverance from sin, efficiency in service, and effectiveness in witnessing are given with the fullness of the Pentecostal blessing. Power to move the world for God and to win souls for Him is neither intellectual nor social, but is in the fullness of the Spirit of God in the soul. "Ye shall receive power after that the Holy Ghost is come upon you."

Ye Shall Know . . . Ask . . . Do

The promises of our Lord concerning the Spirit gather around the centers knowledge, prayer, service. In that day "ye shall know," "ye shall ask," "ye shall do." Certainty, prayer, work. Certainty in knowledge, assurance in prayer, power in service.

The fullness of the Spirit brings the certainty of revelation to the soul. The men of Pentecost knew the things of God. No theological instruction could have given Peter the doctrine he preached concerning Christ's life, death, and resurrection. "In that day ye shall know," said Jesus, and when the day came they knew; and they knew the things Jesus had said they should know. They knew the essential relationship between Christ and God. The mystery baffles all investigation, but it was made known to them when the Spirit of the Lord "sat upon each of them." They knew the mysterious union of the believer with Christ—that we are in Christ, as the Son is in the Father. It can never be explained, but there is no uncertainty in the knowledge. The secret is disclosed to the heart, and no one sees the writing but the soul that receives it. They know that Christ is also in the believer as surely as the Christ and the Father are one. There are no words in the Bible quite so profound as these seven tiny words, "Ye in Me, and I in you"; but the gift of Pentecost reveals their mystery and establishes their certainty. The Spirit-filled KNOW. They have knowledge that does not depend upon intellectual capacity, scholarly training, or even on experience, and their certainty is the secret of their power. They have knowledge that comes not of flesh and blood but from the Spirit who knows the deep things of God, for He is Himself God. And the Spirit not only reveals the deep things of God but gives also illumination for all the practical affairs of life. All questions are answered in Him. The Spirit-filled are not left in uncertainty as to the mind of God. Pentecost brings a pervasive light, according to the words in 1 John 2:27: "The anointing which ye received of Him abideth in you, and ye need not that anyone teach you; but as His anointing teacheth you concerning all things, and is true, and is no lie, and even as it taught you, ye abide in Him."

The Pentecostal blessing makes the believer

mighty in prayer. "In that day ye shall ask in My name
... and whatsoever ye shall ask the Father in My name
He will give you." Prayer is an impossible task without
the Holy Ghost. We know not what we should pray
for as we ought, but the Spirit helpeth our infirmities.
There are two kinds of praying. Before Pentecost we
pray in the Spirit; after Pentecost the Spirit prays
through us. "He maketh intercession for us with
groanings that cannot be uttered." None but the Spirit-
filled know that kind of praying. It is the kind that
wrought miracles in the Acts of the Apostles, and to
this day prevails. It pleads the Name, enthrones the
Name, and claims the Name. It prays in His will,
presents His promise, and decrees in His power. Prayer
brings Pentecost, and Pentecost makes prayer omni-
potent for all the will of God. The Spirit instructs and
inspires prayer, gives intelligence and intensity to
intercession, and brings reality and joy to communion
with God. The Spirit-filled love to pray, and prayer
that is in the Spirit must prevail.

Pentecost is always associated with power. The
final promise of our Lord was "Ye shall receive power
after that the Holy Ghost is come upon you." The
Spirit of God is the Spirit of Power. Everywhere in
the Scriptures He is associated with the might of
Almighty God. In the Old Testament He wrought
mightily, even though "He was not yet given." In the
New Testament He is God's crowning gift of Power.
He clothes Himself with sanctified men and women,
"that the excellency of the power may be of God, and
not of us." The measure of our power is in the energy
of the Holy Spirit, working in us and through us. All

fullness of life, all resources of vitality, all certainty of assurance, all victory over sin and the flesh, all prevailing power in prayer, all certitude of glory—all and everything is in the indwelling Presence and power of the Holy Spirit of God in Christ Jesus our Lord.

The Inheritance of the Spirit-Filled

Romans 8 is the fullest exposition of the life which comes through "the Spirit of Life in Christ Jesus." It is the charter of the believer's inheritance in the Spirit.

(1) *Pentecost Brings Deliverance*

The law of the Spirit of Life in Christ Jesus makes men free. Where the Spirit of the Lord is, there is liberty. He is the Spirit of Power, and the first demonstration of power is emancipation. He breaks the power of canceled sin. There is no bondage from which He cannot deliver. He breaks the fetters of the soul and opens the prison doors of the redeemed. Salvation comes with the suddenness of a mighty rushing wind and as with the flash of fire; or it may come as the breath of the morning and the light of the dawn. However it comes, it comes to set men free from all that brings into bondage and condemnation. It is the gospel of liberty to all imprisoned life. There is no slave the gospel cannot save. The greatest deliverance of all is from the moral impotence of the dual personality of chapter 7. The measure of completeness is in the word: "There is therefore now no condemnation to them that are in Christ Jesus." They are delivered from all and everything that brings condemnation.

(2) *Pentecost Brings Abounding Vitality*

Our Lord came that we might have abundant and abounding life, and it is found in the gift of the Spirit of Life. The gift of God is living water, springing up into everlasting life. Living water is the water of vitality from the eternal Source of Life. The law is good, but weak through the flesh, ineffective through human infirmity. The Holy Spirit strengthens the inward man. The Spirit of Life dwells in men, permeates their being, sanctifies their nature, quickens their powers, vitalizes their mortal bodies, and radiates their life. They live—really live! They live the life that is life indeed. Pentecost turned anemic believers into exuberant saints. People said they were drunk, and so they were, but not with wine. They were vivacious with abounding vitality. Pentecost wakens people up. It vitalizes latent powers and makes the utmost of every faculty and gift. Those who would have Life—abounding Life, victorious Life, satisfying Life, glorious Life—must get to Pentecost. Life is the best medicine for every kind of sickness. It cures all ills, ends all weariness, and conquers death all the time.

(3) *Pentecost Brings Understanding*

Where did Peter get the sermon he preached on the Day of Pentecost? He did not read it from a carefully prepared manuscript. This fisherman Apostle is always surprising us with the things he knows. Who taught him? How did he know the hidden meaning of prophecy? How did he come to understand the philosophy of history so that he could say with certainty, "This is that"? How came he to understand the meaning of the Cross and to discover the explanation of the resurrection of Jesus from the dead? Who instructed him in these things? The Master tells how he had come to know that He was the Christ the Son of God—and that one explanation explains the rest. He knew by the Spirit of Wisdom and Revelation. The Spirit of Truth guides into all truth. "In that day ye shall KNOW." We know by the Spirit that we are sons of God and joint heirs with Christ.

The Spirit Himself is our witness. We know that the world is redeemed, and therefore travails in hope, waiting for its redemption through "the revealing of the Sons of God"—a new creation by regeneration. We know, and do not despair. "We know that to them that love God all things work together for good, even to them that are called according to His purpose." We know, and are not as others in the day of adversity. We know God. We know, and we know that we know. We know that at the last we shall be saved, and shall stand approved in Christ at the Throne of God. None shall lay anything to the charge of God's elect. Nothing shall separate us from the love of God which is in Christ Jesus. "In that Day ye shall know." The Spirit is familiar with the deep things of God, and He takes of the things of Christ and reveals them unto those who receive Him. He is the Spirit of Wisdom as well as of Revelation. He leads in practical wisdom as well as guides into all truth. He makes men wise with the wisdom that is from above.

(4) *Pentecost Brings a New Fellowship in Prayer*

"And in like manner the Spirit also helpeth our

infirmity: for we know not how to pray as we ought; but the Spirit Himself maketh intercession for us with groanings that cannot be uttered; and He that searcheth the hearts knoweth what is the mind of the Spirit, because He maketh intercession for the saints according to the will of God." That is the secret of prevailing prayer.

(5) *Pentecost Brings Power*

That was the specific promise of Christ. "Ye shall receive power after that the Holy Ghost is come upon you, and ye shall be witnesses unto Me." Witnessing prevails over the enemy. "We are more than conquerors," says St. Paul, and St. John ascribes the victory to testimony. "And they overcame him [Satan] because of the blood of the Lamb, and because of the word of their testimony; and they loved not their lives unto death" (Rev. 12:11). The Spirit of Power is given for witnessing. The testimony of Pentecost was mighty. It is always mighty in the demonstration of the Spirit.

(6) *Pentecost Brings the Fire of God*

Fire is the chosen symbol of heaven for moral passion. It is emotion aflame. God is love; God is fire. The two are one. The Holy Spirit baptizes in fire. Spirit-filled souls are ablaze for God. They love with a love that glows. They believe with a faith that kindles. They serve with a devotion that consumes. They hate sin with a fierceness that burns. They rejoice with a joy that radiates. Love is perfected in the Fire of God. Nothing can separate us from the love of God.

(7) *Pentecost Brings Passion for the Souls of Men*

The eighth chapter overflows into the ninth. The experience consummates in anguish of tears for the lost. There is no sterner test of grace than the attitude toward the lost. Pentecost leads back to Gethsemane, for it baptizes into Christ's Baptism of Redeeming Passion. Spirit-filled hearts are always tender, and they see men through the tears of a holy compassion.

7

The Indwelling Spirit

INWARDNESS is the distinctive feature of the Spirit. The Son of God reveals and works from without, but the Spirit of God dwells and works from within. The Son is the Word. He reveals the living and eternal truth and is the express image of the invisible and glorious God. The Spirit is the secret Presence. He is the source of life and truth; the very soul of the universe, and the source of light and life, wisdom and power. He is behind the Word, within the strength, the Dweller in the innermost of all secret places.

In all the Old Testament references to the Spirit there is the suggestion of inwardness. At the Creation, God made the heavens and the earth, but the Spirit is said to have brooded over the face of the waters, as if He would beget rather than create. The Son is said to have made the worlds, but there is no suggestion of the Son brooding over creation. When God threatened to destroy the world for its wickedness, He said, "My Spirit shall not always strive with man." Striving implies an inward contest rather than an outward compulsion. From within He sought to instruct, correct and save. Again, when God chose Israel to be His peculiar people, Nehemiah says, "Thou gavest also Thy Good Spirit to instruct them." The instruction covered a wide area, from Bezaleel, the craftsman, who was filled "with the Spirit of God, in wisdom, and in understanding, and in knowledge, and in all manner of workmanship," to the prophets, who "spake as they were moved by the Holy Ghost." There is one marginal reading in the Revised Version that is both emphatic and illuminating: "The Spirit of the Lord clothed Itself with Gideon" (Judg. 6:34). He did not come upon him like a garment, but the Spirit clothed Himself with Gideon as with a garment.

From "With" to "In"

The distinction is patent enough in the New Testament. The very first word of promise concerning the Spirit in the Upper Room emphasizes it. "Ye know him; for He abideth with you, and shall be in you." The change from *with* to *in* marks the transition from one dispensation to another. The very essence of the Christian religion is in the realized Presence of God in the soul, and his Presence is the Pentecostal gift of the Spirit. There is often some confusion in the interchange of terms, and the elimination of the middle factor. The Son comes in the coming of the Spirit, and abides in the soul in the presence of the Spirit; and in the coming of the Son through the Spirit the Father comes and abides also. "He will come . . . I will come . . . We will come" all refer to the coming of the Spirit as promised in our Lord's farewell talk with His disciples (John 14:16–23). "In their relation to the human soul the Father and the Son act through and are represented by the Holy Spirit. And yet the Spirit is not merged in either the Father or in the Son." There is absolute unity with perfect distinction of Persons in the Trinity. They are never confused in the unity nor divided in the distinction. Each is divine and all are one.

The Spirit works from within. That is the distinction that makes all the difference. There were things Christ could not do that are possible to the Spirit for this very reason. *"He that abideth with you shall dwell in you"*; and so it came to pass. "The Holy Spirit which dwelleth in us." Auguste Sabatier says: "It is not enough to represent the Spirit of God as coming as a help for man's spirit, supplying strength which he lacks—an associate or juxtaposed force, a supernatural auxiliary. . . . There is no simple addition of divine power to human power in the Christian life. The Spirit of God identifies Himself with the human *me* into which it enters and whose life it becomes. If we may so speak, it is individualized in the new moral personality it creates." The Spirit of God identified with the human *me*; the human *me* identified with the Spirit of God. The Spirit of God is the Spirit of Christ, and the experience of Galatians 2:20 is the result. That is as our Lord promised. He that is with you shall be in you. "I in you, and ye in Me."

The Spirit in the Son

Paul singles out the fact of our Lord's resurrection

to set forth the work of the Spirit in the mediatorial work of the Son. He selects the resurrection because it was the culminating and representative act, but the same Spirit was in all our Lord's life and ministry. The indwelling Spirit is the key to both His personality and His work. When He became man He emptied Himself of all the prerogatives and privileges of deity. He Himself was unchanged, for He is the same yesterday, today and forever, but He laid aside all that belonged to His exalted state and submitted to the limitations of our nature and our lot. But God gave to the self-emptied Son the fullness of His Spirit, and our Lord was in all things dependent upon the Spirit. His body was prepared for Him by the Spirit. He grew in wisdom and in stature under the guidance of the Spirit. His teaching was given to Him by the Spirit, and His miracles were wrought in the power of the Spirit. At the last He offered Himself to God through the eternal Spirit, and it was the Spirit that brought again our Lord Jesus from the dead. The standard of the Spirit's power is demonstrated in the Son. He is the Spirit's unit of measurement; the standard and sample of what the Holy Ghost can do in and for and through sanctified humanity.

The Spirit in the Believer

The believer's fellowship with the Son is as absolute as the Son's fellowship with the Father. He has no more reserves in His partnership than in His renunciation. He has made possible to *us* whatever was or is accessible to *Him*. The gift of His Spirit includes all His inheritance just as the Father gave all in His Son. "He shall be *in* you." The very same Spirit that was in Him shall be in *us*. All that He had been to Him He comes to be to us. The Spirit dwells in the believer as He dwelt in the Son. There is no other interpretation to be put on such sayings as these:

> "Know ye not that your body is the temple of the Holy Ghost which is in you?" (1 Cor. 6:19).
> "Ye are the temple of the living God; as God hath said, I will dwell in them, and walk in them" (2 Cor. 6:16).
> "Ye are not in the flesh, but in the Spirit, if so be that the Spirit of God dwelleth in you" (Rom. 8:9).
> "But if the Spirit of Him that raised up Jesus from the dead dwelleth in you, He that raised up Christ Jesus from the dead shall quicken also your mortal bodies through His Spirit that dwelleth in you" (Rom. 8:11).

What does it mean exactly to say "He dwelleth in you"?

Christian teachers are often disposed to interpret the language of the Scriptures here as a strong figure of speech. Dying with Christ, fellowship in His resurrection, and the mutual indwelling of the believer and our Lord are attempts to express the experience of the soul in its relation to spiritual life and power. They argue that these expressions are not to be taken literally, but as types of great spiritual realities in the soul. What saith the Scripture? The New Testament abounds with teaching and testimony that demand a deeper explanation. If the terms used do not involve personality, there is an end of intelligible speech. The indwelling is that of a real, personal, spiritual Presence.

It is not a gift that can be located somewhere in the brain or heart of a man, but a personal Spirit that indwells another personality; a personality within a personality by which the Spirit becomes the life of my life, the soul of my soul; an indwelling that secures identity without confusion and possession without absorption. "He that is Christ's not merely has the Spirit of Christ ruling in him, leading him, guiding him, sanctifying him, preparing him body and soul for glorification; but has Him also as the new animating Soul of his soul, Spirit of his spirit, repeating in himself the mystery of the union of two natures in one personality."

That is the mystery of grace that passeth all understanding, and the miracle of grace by which the incarnation is perpetuated in the Body of Christ. That is the mystery of the ages. "In that day ye shall know that I am in My Father, and ye in Me, and I in you" (John 14:20). Of course it is a mystery; a truth that can never be discovered and is known only by revelation. What is promised transcends human achievement and human understanding. "It is a work of divine omnipotence and love. The gift of the Holy Ghost is the most personal act of the Godhead. It is the goodness of God alone that must give it. It is His omnipotence that must work it in us. The blessing of Pentecost is a supernatural gift, a wonderful act of God in the soul. It is an unspeakably holy and glorious thing that a man can be filled with the Spirit of God."

The Incarnation of the Spirit

The marginal reading of Judges 6:34 (Revised Version) will help us here again, especially if we read it in the light of New Testament experience: "the Spirit clothed Himself with Gideon." Spirit clothing itself with humanity is the miracle of incarnation. A body is as necessary to the Spirit as to the Son. For the Son a body was prepared by the Spirit; for the Spirit a body is made possible by the Son. The Spirit lived in and through Gideon. The life of Gideon became the life of the Spirit. The man was endued and the Spirit was clothed. The Spirit thought through Gideon's brain, felt through Gideon's heart, looked through Gideon's eyes, spoke through Gideon's voice, wrought by Gideon's hands, and yet all the time Gideon was still Gideon and the Spirit was still the Spirit.

The same Spirit quickens our mortal bodies by dwelling in them. Romans 8:11 is a *present* experience. Calvin says that by "mortal bodies" Paul means "whatever remains in us that is still liable to death. The customary usage is to apply this term to the more material part of us; therefore the word is used, not of the final resurrection, which takes place in a moment, but of the *continual* operation of the Spirit, which, quickening the flesh, sets up the heavenly life within us." The Spirit who dwells in us quickens our mortal bodies. This does not create new faculties, but it awakens the dormant and develops the latent. The natural endowments of a man are the basis of the Spirit's energy, but there is no part of a man's being that is not vitalized and strengthened by His power.

The Spirit gives fullness of life. He gives health as surely as He gives life. There is truth at the back of all the vagaries of health movements in the name of the Christian faith, and fear of extremes must not be allowed to frighten us from the truth. Sickness may be and is in the will of God for some of His children, but even in them strength is made perfect in weakness. Faith health is better than faith healing, and the quickening Spirit makes for vitality and vigor as surely as He makes for sanity and spiritual power.

The Spirit redeems the material through the spiritual. Creation groans for deliverance through the Spirit, and for social redemption there is no other way of salvation. The Spirit dwells in men, clothes Himself with consecrated humanity, and accomplishes extraordinary things through quite ordinary people on the simple conditions of abiding surrender, implicit obedience, and simple faith.

8

The Communion of the Holy Ghost

COMMUNION means "part-nership." The word passes through various phases in the New Testament and is variously translated, but the idea of *sharing* runs through them all. In Luke 5:10, it is said that James and John, sons of Zebedee, were partners with Simon. Paul says of Titus (2 Cor. 8:23) that he was his partner and fellow laborer; that is, they were colleagues in the ministry of the Church. Of Philemon and Onesimus it is used in the still more intimate sense of comradeship. The communion of the Holy Ghost, therefore, means that we are partners, colleagues, comrades with the Spirit of God. We are partners in *vocation* and *resources*, sharers in work and power.

Such communion involves "communication"—that is, intentional sharing. The partners contribute to the common purse for the common good. The New Testament insists upon this grace of fellowship in the Church. The Christians at Philippi are commended because they communicated with the Apostle in the matter of giving and receiving (Phil. 4:15–16), and the Romans are exhorted "to communicate to the necessities of the saints" (Rom. 12:13). The rich are charged "that they do good, that they be rich in good works, that they be ready to distribute, willing to communicate" (1 Tim. 6:18). This idea of partnership is carried into the highest aspects of our calling. We are called by God "into the fellowship of His Son Jesus Christ our Lord" (1 Cor. 1:9); we are "partakers of His sufferings and His comfort" (2 Cor. 1:4–7; Phil. 3:10); and through Him we "become partakers of the divine nature" (2 Pet. 2:4). In all these senses the Holy Spirit of God enters into partnership with us and becomes to us colleague and comrade, sharing what we have, and admitting us into His mission and placing at our disposal all the resources of His Person and power.

Our Fellowship and His

Emphasis is laid upon the fact that He enters into partnership with us rather than that He takes us into partnership with Him. Both aspects are true, for all fellowship must be mutual, but it is never said that our fellowship is with the Spirit. It is always "the communion of the Holy Ghost be with you." In Philippians 2:1, it is "fellowship of the Spirit," and not "with" Him. John says "Our fellowship is with the Father, and with His Son Jesus Christ" (1 John 1:3). There is no mention of fellowship with the Spirit, and yet "communion" is the special function and distinction of the Spirit. The omission implies that there is a difference between our fellowship with the Father and the Son and the communion of the Holy Ghost with us. "In the one case we are partakers with Christ; in the other the Holy Ghost is partaker with us. This may possibly be connected with the special intimacy of His communion by which He, as a Spirit, enters into the deepest and closest relation with our spirits. That is the first form in which we know it; but thereafter there is a reflex fellowship which we come to have with Him. He enters at first into our position, because He fills our heart and sympathizes with all our need. He then leads us to enter into His position; but that is a higher thing."

This distinction makes plain many things. The Christian Benediction ascribes love to the Father, grace to the Son, and communion to the Holy Ghost. These qualities are common to all the Persons of the Trinity, but distinctive of each. Love is attributed to the Son and Spirit as well as to the Father. Grace is of God the Father as well as of the Son; and our fellowship is expressly said to be with the Father and the Son. There is a distinction, however, that must not be confused. The love of the Father is the origin of grace; the grace of the Lord Jesus Christ is the medium of redeeming love; and through the Spirit is communicated both the grace of the Son and the love of the Father. The Spirit is the executive agent of the Father and the Son. He brings us into the fellowship of the Father and the Son by entering into communion with us. The range of our experience of love and grace is therefore determined by the measure of His communion with us. His partnership with us is progressive, and often His progress is hindered because we admit Him into partnership with qualifications: there are reserves of mind and heart and life. His communion is with us. He seeks to come into cooperation with us. The negotiations are from *Him*, the consent is with *us*. There are no reserves with Him. He is straitened in *us*, for all His negotiations wait for *our* consent.

The Fellowship of the Spirit in the Church

This distinction is observed in all the teaching of our Lord concerning the Spirit. He is the Paraclete, sent by the Father and the Son to abide in the Church until the purpose of redeeming love is accomplished in the world. For all the work of the newly-born Church its members were to look to Him for light and guidance and power. They were sent forth to witness, interpret, and save, but they were first to receive a Witness and Teacher, who is the Spirit of Power. He would be in them and with them. From Him would come the knowledge of the truth about Jesus; by Him they would have the right word at the critical moment; through Him they would do greater works than they had seen Him do. From then until now, the Church is a second body of Christ, prepared and indwelt by the Spirit. In the corporate life of the Church He finds a temple, a medium, and an agent, and in Him the Church finds all its supply of life and grace, wisdom and power.

The basis of His work is always that of communion. That is why the work of the Spirit is always linked with the life of the Church, and the power of the Church is associated with the presence of the Spirit. The Church derives its authority from the Spirit, but the Spirit speaks and works through a praying and consecrated people. The Church that has authority "to bind and to loose" is a Church agreed in prayer and gathered in the Name; and the Church that has power to cast out demons is a Church that believes and prays. The Spirit and the Church cannot be independent of each other. The Spirit needs the Church and the Church needs the Spirit. They are partners—both necessary, and each dependent upon the other. The success of both is according to the measure of "the supply of the Spirit" through the Church to the world. Power is not in organization, neither is it in wealth or learning. It is still true that this work is not by might, nor by power, but by the Spirit of the Lord.

Why, then, is the Church bewildered in the day of confusion and powerless in the presence of both her adversaries and her opportunities? The answer is found in the terms of communion. Conditions exist that make the partnership ineffective. There is "a law of the Spirit" by which His communion is made operative. The laws are few and simple, but they are imperative. He cannot work if they are ignored. Communion must rest on common ground. Its basis is a common bond of union; communion is the outcome of union. In this fellowship the bond is Christ. Where Christ is glorified, the Spirit comes to abide, reveal, direct and work. Through Him we enter into living union with our Lord, for the Spirit of Christ is the Spirit of God, and by Him we find the unity which brings identity of interest and community of possession. That is why faith and prayer count for so much in the work of the Spirit. Nothing else really matters. These are the things that make possible the fellowship of the Spirit. He asks for nothing more than unreserved consecration to Christ, unclouded simplicity of the open heart, and exultant faith in His grace and power. By these the local bodies live and prevail through the fellowship of the Spirit.

The Fellowship of the Spirit in the Believer

The Apostolic Benediction prays: "The communion of the Holy Ghost be with you all." All the blessings of communion are for each believer. There is nothing promised to the Church that does not belong to its humblest member. The Spirit of God is not the monopoly of any particular class. There is nothing done by a minister that may not be done by anyone to whom the Holy Spirit is given. Let that be quite clear. Everyone can say: "The Holy Ghost comes into partnership with me. He is my Helper, my Witness, my Teacher, my Guide, my Strength." For all the will of God we each have the Spirit with all His resources of wisdom and power. All things are possible to the soul strengthened with His might and led in His wisdom. If these things be true, wherein lies the explanation of our weakness and reproach? Where is the note of certainty in our testimony? Where is the prevailing power of prayer? Where is the power that overturns strongholds and casts out forces of evil?

The communion of the Spirit is *with us*. He seeks partnership *with us*. His resources are inexhaustible and His power invincible—but! but! but! There are reserves, conditions, interests; barriers that hinder, grieve and quench the Spirit. He is held up by the barriers of unbelief and prayerless living, of worldly ambition, stupid vanity and inflated pride. He longs for our fellowship. For the sake of Christ and the Kingdom of Grace, He longs to be admitted to confidence and cooperation. He wants a central place in our hearts and to be admitted to the life of the soul. He comes to cooperate, and cooperation waits for confidence and consent. Where there is "agreement" there is power. Service becomes mighty in this fellowship. All the conditions of power are met in "the supply of the Spirit." Personality is quickened and sanctified. Sympathy is deepened and enlightened, and in sympathy are the discernment that understands and the appeal that woos and wins. Weakness becomes strength when the Spirit of Might comes upon us. Ordinary men become wonderful when clothed with the Spirit of Power.

Weakness is a reproach when such a might is at our service. Defeat is dishonor when the partnership of God is rejected. With the communion of the Holy Ghost at our command, what manner of men we ought to be! With such a partnership, what mighty works we ought to do! There are no limits to His power. There are no reserves in His communion. There is no respect of persons with Him. Why do we set boundaries to His work, limit His activities, and refuse His appeal? He brings all; let us give all. "The Spirit which He has

planted within us jealously longs for our love." He seeks
to enter into communion with us in all our life, and in
return He will lead us into the communion of all that
He has and is. Sign the deed today, and enter into the
joy and power of the Holy Spirit of God who is the
Spirit of Christ. "The grace of the Lord Jesus Christ,
and the love of God, and the communion of the Holy
Ghost be with you all."

9

"The Spirit of Christ"

THE SPIRIT of the Lord God is also the Spirit of Christ. This is the distinctive teaching of the New Testament. The progress of the Old Testament revelation of the Spirit finally associates the gift of the Spirit with the promise of the Messiah. "The Spirit of the Lord shall rest upon Him, the Spirit of wisdom and understanding, the Spirit of counsel and might, the Spirit of knowledge and of the fear of the Lord" (Isa. 11:2). Jesus Christ claimed that in Him was fulfilled the Messianic prophecy of the Spirit. He opened His ministry at Nazareth with the announcement that the Spirit of the Lord was upon Him. The Synoptic Gospels reveal the Spirit as the unique power in the life of Jesus, and in St. John's Gospel He is in a unique sense the possession of the Christ, the Son of God. In the Acts of the Apostles and the Epistles He is called the Spirit of Jesus, the Spirit of Christ, the Spirit of Jesus Christ; and the Christian Benediction, like the baptismal formula, associates the Spirit with the Father and the Son. He is the Spirit of God, the Spirit of Christ, the Lord the Spirit; and He is known by about twenty-

five other names in the New Testament, but He is the
same Spirit. It is this multiplicity of names and
functions that leads to so much confusion about the
Spirit.

The Indwelling Spirit and the Indwelling Christ

There is confusion in some minds because the New
Testament speaks of the indwelling Presence
sometimes as the Spirit and at other times as Christ.
St. Paul says emphatically, "Christ liveth in me," and
that Christ is in man the hope of glory; and yet with
equal emphasis he tells us we are the temples of the
Holy Ghost. Does the risen Lord live in us or is it the
Spirit of Christ that dwells in our hearts? The
perplexity arises from our imperfect conception of the
Persons in the Trinity. With us personality is divisive
and exclusive. Each is separate from the rest and must
always be a separate personality. Personality in the
Trinity is not exclusive but inclusive, not divisive but
inherent. God was in Christ, and so also was the Spirit.
In each is All and in All is each. The Spirit "proceedeth
from the Father and the Son." The indwelling Presence
of the Son is revealed and realized in the indwelling
Presence of the Spirit. The great "Temple Prayer" of
the Epistle to the Ephesians (3:14–19) includes all the
Persons of the Trinity in the temple of the human
heart. The Spirit strengthens the inner man, the Son
reveals the divine love to the heart, and the Infinite
God fills the whole being with divine fullness of love,
blessedness, and power. As it pleased God that in His
Son should dwell the fullness of the Godhead bodily,

so it has pleased Him that in the dispensation of the Spirit there should dwell in Him the same fullness; and as in the Son the Father and Spirit were revealed, so in the Spirit are the Son and the Father made known in the soul.

It need not surprise us, therefore, if such close intimacy is expressed in terms that are identical and interchangeable; but the careful reader will observe that the personalities are always distinct. Some modern writers take the view that the Spirit is the New Testament designation for the risen Christ, perpetuated by the influence of His Spirit in the world; but the New Testament Scriptures speak of the Holy Spirit as a Person and never merely as an influence. They always speak of *Him* and never of *It*. And the Person of the Christ is never confounded with the Person of the Holy Spirit. The Spirit did not become Christ in the Incarnation, nor does Jesus become the Spirit at Pentecost. In one sense it is true that when the Spirit comes it is Jesus who comes again to dwell and rule in the hearts and lives of men, but though the Presence is identical, the Personalities are always distinct. Moberly has expressed the distinction perhaps as clearly as we may ever hope to get it when he says: "It is not for an instant that the disciples are to have the presence of the Spirit *instead* of the Son. But to have the Spirit is to have the Son."

The Spirit in the Earthly Ministry of Our Lord

Our Lord said very little about the Holy Spirit during the greater part of His ministry. He confessed freely that He spoke and worked not in His *own* power—but except where necessity constrained Him to speak, He was silent concerning the Spirit by whom He taught and wrought. The explanation of His silence comes out when, on the eve of His departure, He begins to speak at length about the Paraclete who would come when He had gone to the Father. The first word shot its revealing light through all the silent years. "Ye know Him, for He abideth with you." Just as seeing Him they had seen the Father, so in knowing Him they had known the Spirit. In Him was the fullness of the Godhead, and as through Him came the revelation of the Father, so by Him was the manifestation of the Spirit. Therein is the key to the Person and work of our Lord.

All themes that lead us into the inter-relations of the Trinity are "hard to be uttered," but the things that are revealed are intended to be understood, and prayer opens the eyes of both mind and heart. It is no part of faith to shrink from a subject because it involves risk and demands great caution, sustained attention, and delicate expression. The emphasis of modern theological thought has been for years upon the *kenosis*, as stated in Philippians 2:5−8. It is contended that by reason of our Lord's self-emptying there remained nothing that distinguished Him essentially from other men. The contention overlooks the fact that there is a *pleroma* as well as a *kenosis*. Our Lord emptied Himself, but the Father gave to His self-emptied Son the fullness of His Spirit. He did not cease to be God, but He became in all things human and was subject to such conditions as were possible to human nature possessed of His Spirit. Through all the earthly life and ministry of our Lord He was indebted to the presence and power of the Holy Ghost.

"The Spirit of Counsel and Might"

Our Lord's life was mapped out for Him. He came to do the Father's will, and that will was unfolded and interpreted to Him by the Holy Spirit. He grew in wisdom as in stature, but it is difficult to mark the stages and boundaries of His knowledge. He was led of the Spirit, taught of the Spirit, and strengthened in the Spirit. He never said "Perhaps" and balanced the probabilities. He never made a mistake. His sagacity never erred, neither did His power fail; and for both He was constantly dependent upon the Spirit that was given without measure.

He spoke the words of God as they were given to Him by the Spirit. Five times in John's Gospel our Lord claims to be speaking under authority:

> "He whom God hath sent speaketh the words of God: for He giveth not the Spirit by measure" (3:34).
>
> "Jesus therefore answered them, and said, My teaching is not Mine, but His that sent Me" (7:16).
>
> "Jesus therefore said, When ye have lifted up the Son of Man, then shall ye know that I am He, and that I do nothing of Myself, but as the Father taught Me, I speak these things" (8:28).
>
> "Believest thou not that I am in the Father, and the Father in Me? The words that I say unto you I speak not from Myself: but the Father abiding in Me

doeth His works. . . . He that loveth Me not keepeth not My words: and the word which ye hear is not Mine, but the Father's who sent Me" (14:10, 24).

The same is true of His ministry of power. His first text linked His ministry with the Messianic promise of the Spirit. He was Spirit-prepared, Spirit-called, Spirit-equipped, and Spirit-sent. He did nothing of Himself any more than for Himself. Speaking in the house of Cornelius, the Apostle Peter thus summarizes and accounts for the life of our Lord: "Even Jesus of Nazareth, how that God anointed Him with the Holy Ghost and with power: who went about doing good, and healing all that were oppressed of the devil; for God was with Him" (Acts 10:38). His miracles were all wrought in the power of the Holy Ghost. Even His atoning death was by the grace of God and through the eternal Spirit (Heb. 2:9; 9:14), and it was by the same Spirit of power that God raised Him from the dead. From the Incarnation to the Resurrection, the life and ministry of Jesus Christ, the Son of God, were lived and wrought in and through and by the power of the Spirit of the Father and the Son. The Spirit of Christ is the Spirit of God. In Christ the Spirit of God becomes the spirit of man in "the Word made Flesh."

It is this truth, so immense in its significance, that is the distinctive revelation of the New Testament and the distinctive note in the life of the Church of Christ. For the Spirit of Pentecost is the Spirit of Christ. The Spirit He gives is the self-same Spirit that inspired, instructed, and animated His own life: His own, very own Spirit, which may be said to be His very self. Jesus calls Him the Paraclete, and assures the distressed disciples that in that day they would know what He could not yet teach them and do greater works than He had done. The Spirit is the all-inclusive gift of the Father to His Son, and the crowning gift of the Son to His people. In a deeper and fuller sense than we have yet realized, the Spirit of God is the Spirit of Christ, and it is in the Spirit of Christ we live the life which is life indeed. The fullness of God is in Christ, and Christ lives in men through His Spirit. He is Himself the gift. He brings all the blessings of grace and wisdom and power, but He is the Blesser and the Blessing. There is in the soul a very true sense of a divinely real Presence. The Spirit makes the Presence real. This is the crowning mystery and glory of grace.

The Christian religion is not a set of doctrines about Christ, neither is it a rule of life based upon the teaching and example of Christ. It is not even an earnest and sincere endeavor to live according to the mind and spirit of Christ. It is *life*, and that life is the life of Christ. It is a continuation of the life of the risen Lord in His Body which is the Church, and in the sanctified believer. "Christ liveth in me" is the essence of the Christian religion as set forth in the New Testament. It is not a system but a Presence: the Spirit of Christ indwelling the spirit of man.

10

"The Spirit of Power"

THERE ARE two words for "power" in the Greek New Testament, one of which denotes *authority* and the other *force*. Much confusion has arisen from the failure to distinguish between them. Just as the two words for "perfection" stand respectively for completeness or for consummation, so the two words for "power" indicate either authority or effectiveness, either right or efficiency. The Revised Version has been more careful to preserve the distinction than the Authorized, but it has not been as successful as might have been expected; for instance, in John 10:18, where our Lord speaks not of His ability but of His *authority* to lay down His life and take it again. Both words are used in Luke 9:1: "He called the twelve together, and gave them power and authority over all devils, and to cure diseases." When the seventy returned with joy, saying, "Lord, even the devils are subject unto us in Thy name, He said, Behold, I give you authority . . . over all the power of the enemy" (Luke 10:17–19).

Man's Instinct for Power

Man wants power. There is probably no instinct of the heart so strong as the craving for the sovereignty of power. Might is the attribute of God most coveted by men. Satan snatched at it and fell, and the same craving was the undoing of the human race. "Ye shall be as God" was the appeal that prevailed; and its success was in the fact that it appealed to the craving for sovereignty. Man was made for thrones and dominion. He knew it. He snatched at it and fell. Even then the instinct for power remained. It is the dominant passion of the human race and the key to its history. The determination to possess it is responsible for more than half the bloodshed of the world, and its urge has been the dynamic of civilization in all ages. The kingdoms of this world are built on the love of power. Babylon stands in the Bible for the symbol of human ambition. The Tower of Babel was to reach to the heavens and make for its people a name that would endure forever.

> "Thou saidst in thine heart, I will ascend into heaven, I will exalt my throne above the stars of God; and I will sit upon the mount of congregation, in the uttermost parts of the earth. I will ascend above the heights of the clouds; I will be like the Most High."

Babylon is not a geographical term, and its spirit is still with us.

Man was meant for the heights. God made him for sovereignty, and he cannot fulfill his destiny without power. God destined him for a throne; Satan promised him a kingdom. The difference between God's purpose and Satan's promise is a difference of method and purpose. The kingdoms were not the same. Neither was the way the same. God's way is the way of grace; Satan's is that of lawlessness. God brings it as a gift, for which man must wait in patient obedience and humble trust; Satan bids man snatch at it, demand it as a right, and take it. The devil's doctrine has always been that might is right. No authority must stand between man and his will. Animal instinct, the gratification of desire, the passion to have and to know, are declared to be the only justification man needs for taking what he wants, provided he has the power. Satan's way to thrones and dominion is by the assertion of self for self-realization; God's way is by the surrender of self on the altar of sacrifice. Calvary is God's way. In the Kingdom of Heaven the bleeding Lamb is in the midst of the Throne, and in the midst of everything else that abides. The way of sovereignty is by the way of the Cross. The badge of authority is service, the mark of distinction is humility, and the right to rule is the power to obey. God's way gets there. The other ends in the ditch and the pit.

The Promise of Power

Man needs power. He is of no use without it. Dominion is impossible without authority, and authority is useless without power. Man must have power. It is his supreme need. Without power he can do nothing. He needs it for both character and inheritance. He cannot be what he was made to be, and he cannot do what he ought to do, without the right to command and the power to accomplish. The gift of power was the last promise of our Lord and the first declaration of the Spirit.

> "Ye shall receive power after that the Holy Ghost is come upon you."

Our Lord promised that the indwelling Presence of the Spirit of God would be in men the all-prevailing source of power. The Spirit of God is always associated with energy and vitality. He brooded over the chaos of the world and brought it into order and under control. He was God's gift to man at his creation, and it was "the Breath of God" that distinguished man from the rest of His creatures. During the period recorded in the Old Testament Scriptures, the Spirit was given to men chosen for special tasks. The prophets foresaw an age in which He would be poured forth upon all flesh and spoke of His coming. Jesus manifested the Spirit as He revealed the Father. By His promise the Spirit was to succeed the Son with increased effectiveness and enlarged dominion. For that reason it was better that He should go away.

The gift of the Spirit is God's gift of power for effective witnessing, holiness of life, and consecrated service. It gives authority, aptness, and force in speech. On the Day of Pentecost men spoke as the Spirit of God gave them utterance. They spoke with authority, certainty and power, because they spoke out of an experience of revealed truth interpreted by the Holy Ghost. The power of the keys follows a divine revelation of God in Christ, and no man has a right to speak for God who has no personal, firsthand knowledge of Him: he certainly will not speak with power. The Spirit of Power sanctifies, vitalizes, energizes the natural faculties, and makes possible things beyond their most perfect development. God's man becomes mighty in the power of the Almighty. Personality is the seat of power, and the Pentecostal gift of the Spirit is the gift of a God-possessed personality.

Power in Personality

The gift of the Spirit is a gift of personality. It turns ordinary persons into extraordinary personalities. That is the miracle of Pentecost.

Personality is the discovery of the age. It is not easy to define, but there is a certain currency of ideas and words that give it high rank in all modern thinking. It is meant to imply more than a person. It is a person of distinctive quality. Remarkably enough, the New Testament never uses the word. God asks for persons, and turns them into personalities. It is a quality that counts. "For Shamgar slew six hundred Philistines with an oxgoad, and saved Israel; but the men of Ephraim, being armed, and carrying bows, turned back in the day of battle." The reason was not in the weapons but in the men. Personality is the supreme power. Superior to heredity, stronger than environment, higher than prestige, mightier than adversity, a man's personality conquers, compels, commands. It gives distinction in art, effectiveness to energy, and character to life. In all the work of the world it is personality that counts, and everywhere it is held that the qualities of powerful personality are courage, strength, sympathy, and sanity. Not one of them can be spared, and I do not know that the order can be changed.

Now "God hath not given us the Spirit of fear; but of power, and of love, and of a sound mind." The gift of the Spirit is a gift of personality that possesses man's spirit, quickens man's faculties, sanctifies man's powers, and empowers him for all the will of God.

The Bible nowhere uses the word "personality." (It is difficult to imagine how it could be written without the word, but it was.) God never asks for personalities. With us they are the first condition in all enterprises that call for power. There is, however, no divine quest for supermen. God asks for persons. He calls all sorts of people and chooses quite ordinary men and women for His great work. He somehow calls persons and makes them personalities. He gives power. Our Lord said to His disciples: "Behold, I send forth the promise of My Father upon you: tarry ye in the city, until ye be clothed with power from on high."

To be "clothed" means something more than to be covered. The Holy Spirit of God clothes Himself with sanctified humanity, and in Him sanctified humanity is properly clothed. The Spirit fits in with every element of personality, gives power of expression to every faculty, shines in illuminating power upon every theme in reason, conscience and heart, and brings to pass the ideals, desires, and purposes of God in heart and life. Every kind of power comes in the Spirit: intellectual power, moral power, spiritual power and physical power. That is the Personality of Pentecost. There is no higher quality of man anywhere, and he can be produced everwhere by the power of the Holy Ghost. He is the Spirit of Truth, the Spirit of Holiness, and the Spirit of Power. He quickens the mind, purifies the heart, and strengthens the whole man.

Power! Power belongs to God, and in the gift of the Spirit He makes all grace abound to us, that we, having all-sufficiency in all things, may abound unto every good work. Power! All things are possible for those who have power. Power! The supreme need of man and the crowning gift of God is power: power to conquer, power to attain, power to achieve. The Spirit of God is the Spirit of Power.

The Laws of Power

All power is conditioned. A very little thing will stop a motorcar, silence thousands of spindles, or plunge a city into darkness. Spiritual power, likewise, is subject to conditions. Once it failed in the hands of the Apostles. The same chapter in Luke that tells of its gift tells how they tried to cast out an evil spirit from a demoniac lad and could not.

The power of the Spirit is inseparable from His Person. God does not let out His attributes. His power cannot be rented. It cannot be detached from His presence. He strengthens by indwelling. Spirit works through spirit. He is not simply the Giver of power, He wields it. No one else can. It is His power working in us that makes us all-powerful for all the will of God. Is it not in this we so often fail? Is there not often in our praying for power more desire for *it* than for *Him*?

Is it not possible to be more anxious for the achievements of power than for the Spirit of Power? We want visible results, dramatic wonders, mighty works; and it is not always for these that the Spirit of Power is given. Power may be as necessary for silence as for speech, and as mighty in obscurity as in high places. He comes to make us effective in all the will of God. In the one Spirit there are diversities both of function and manifestation.

The work of the Spirit depends upon the power of the Spirit. No other power will do. The energy of the flesh cannot do the work of the Spirit. For His power there is no substitute. When Zion covets Babylonish gold, envies Babylonish garments, copies Babylonish ways, adopts Babylonish altars, and fights with Babylonish weapons, her strength fails because the Spirit of Power is lost. Carnal resources are no asset in spiritual enterprise. The weapons of this warfare are not carnal. Prayer brings power, for the Spirit of Power is given to them that pray. Testimony is a chosen weapon of conquest, and the Spirit is given for witnessing. He does not save by argued abstractions, but by living witnesses who testify with power out of the personal certainty of a living experience. It is by the power of the Spirit that there comes conviction of sin, righteousness, and judgment. The work of the Church is supernatural. It cannot be done in the strength of the natural man. "It is not by might, nor by power, but by My Spirit, saith the Lord." There is no excuse for failure, no justification for ineffectiveness, for the Spirit of God is the Spirit of Power, and the gift of the Spirit is the inheritance of every believer in Christ Jesus our Lord. "He that is feeble among them at that day shall be as David; and the House of David shall be as God, as the Angel of the Lord before them."

Where Is the Spirit of Power?

The atmosphere of the Apostolic Church is charged with divine power. Their word was with power. Conviction accompanied their speech. Signs and wonders confirmed their testimony. They uncovered the hearts of evil doers, and Heaven put its seal upon their judgments. Rulers trembled in their presence. The dead heard their voice. Disease fled at their touch. Demons were subject to their word. The presence of the Spirit endued men with divine authority and power. They were sure of the mind of God, for they were taught by the Spirit. They asked and received, for they prayed in the Spirit. They wrought mighty works, for they were strengthened in the might of the Spirit. The normal life of the Church was filled, inspired, and empowered in the fullness of the Spirit of the living God.

The study of Pentecost reveals a startling contrast between the promise of power and its absence in the Church of today.

Judged by its own standards of power, the Church is not effectively doing its own proper work. This is the conviction of devout and thoughtful men in all the churches. Why? Where is now the Lord God of Elijah? Where is the Spirit of Power that raised the dead, cleansed the lepers, cast out evil spirits, and transformed men into saints and heroes of God? So far as external conditions can be judged, they are more favorable to the work of the Spirit than they have been for many years. There is a revolt against materialism and rationalism. There is an intense belief in the reality of the spiritual world. All these things have opened a great and effectual door to the witness of the Holy Spirit of God; and yet the Church has less power than in the days of aggressive antagonism. Why? Is the Spirit of the Lord straitened? Forsyth, as usual, puts his finger on the spot when he says: "The arrest of the Church's extensive effect is due to the decay of its intensive faith, while a mere piety muffles the loss." There is no substitute for the Holy Ghost. The sufficiency of the Church is not of men, but of God. The one vital cause of failure in the Church is in the poverty of the spiritual life of its people.

As the Holy Spirit was straitened in the human body and earthly ministry of our Lord, so is He straitened today in the Church which is His Body—with a difference. There then were words the Spirit could not yet speak and works He could not yet do, but there were no limitations of unbelief, unresponsiveness or disobedience in Christ; whereas in the modern Church there are conditions that make His work difficult and sometimes impossible.

All the causes of our failure go back to this one common source: Do we believe in the Holy Ghost, the Spirit of Truth, the Lord and Giver of Life? Is it not true that there are many who have not so much as heard that the Holy Ghost has been given? Without His guidance wisdom gropes in darkness, and without

His strength there is no might. Light becomes darkness, and strength weakness, apart from Him. There are many who would save the Church by linking it up with the powers of the world. Christ was the Good Physician who healed by the Spirit of Life, but the modern Saviour is an Engineer who will redeem by organization and accommodation. The salvation of the world is "not by might, nor by power, but by My Spirit, saith the Lord of Hosts." There is no straitening in Him. The reason for our failure is not in Him. He is straitened in us. Is He straitened in me?

11

"The Spirit of Life"

TRUTH and life are the distinctive features of the Spirit emphasized in the Nicene Creed. He is said to be the Lord and Giver of life . . . who spake by the prophets. The Lord and Giver of life! Our Lord said that He was the Life, and the Spirit is said to be the Spirit of Life, just as our Lord is the Truth and the Spirit is the Spirit of Truth. The Eternal Word, the Living Spirit, and the Tongue of Fire are a trinity in the unity of the revealed Word; and so it is with the creation, lordship, and perfecting of life. Our life is in Christ. It is in Him, and from Him, and by Him, and to Him. "In Him was life." "For as the Father hath life in Himself, even so gave He to the Son to have life in Himself." He came that through Him men might have life, and have it abundantly. Life is the gift of God in Christ Jesus. The Divine Spirit is the Spirit of Life.

The Lord and Giver of Life

All life is due to the direct action of the Spirit of God. He is its medium and its Lord. The phrase "Spirit of Life" is a comprehensive phrase indicating His relation to all life. By Him came the life of the world. Through all the seasons and millenniums, the earth has been renewed and replenished by the eternal and living Spirit of God. To Him the Bible attributes the whole life of man. From Him is every intellectual and artistic gift, every emotional and volitional capacity, every gift of grace and love. The Spirit is associated with the whole man. Apart from Him men are dead. It is the coming of the Spirit that gives true life.

That He is the Spirit of Life cannot mean less than that He is the life-giving Spirit. It cannot mean less than that in the Spirit of the living God is the Source, Medium, and Agent of living energy, the expression of revealed truth, the secret of divine power, and every other quality and function of life. The source and seat of all life is in and through Him, for all life is of the Spirit. The Spirit is the Giver of life, and where the Spirit is not, there is no life. Life has been defined by the scientists as the dynamical condition of an organism, but the definition confuses more than it makes plain. Life is, in its essence, of the Spirit, spiritual. It is more than a dynamic, separate from conditions, and distinct from its organism. Life is in itself spirit, and the true life is from the Spirit of Life. It is more than existence, for the Bible speaks of those who are dead while they live. Life has its seat in man's spiritual nature—in his self-conscious reason, his moral sense, and his capacity for the knowledge of and fellowship with God. Life is more than animal existence, just as death is more than physical dissolution. The Spirit of God quickens into life the spirit of man. The body of man is the temple of the Holy Ghost, but He does not dwell in the flesh. Spirit dwells in spirit. The Spirit of God dwells in the spirit of man; and from that center of life and power He quickens, directs, controls, and sanctifies the whole man. He indwells sanctified men and women. He becomes the spirit of their spirit, the mind of their mind, the heart of their heart, the strength of their strength, and the life of their life.

The sphere of the Spirit is in the realm of life. He gives the life that is in Christ, and in all things He works through the law of the Spirit of Life. He works and fashions the outward from the inward, and the material through the spiritual. He functions through life.

The Spirit giveth life, and the Spirit working through the life strengthens, directs, and transforms. He reveals the face of Christ and transforms us into the same image, from glory to glory, even as from the Lord the Spirit. All understanding of the truth as it is in Jesus is by the Lord and Giver of life who spoke by the prophets, and He is given to guide believers into all the truth. All Christlikeness of life and character is by the transforming power of life through the Spirit of the living God, the Lord and Giver of life. That is why the work of God in the Church depends upon the life of the Church. The City of the living God comes through the Spirit of the living God. That is why an ecclesiastical dignitary may know less about conversion than a Hallelujah lass of the Salvation Army! That is why spiritual power is so often in inverse ratio to scholastic accomplishments! It is not by might of carnal strength, nor in the power of organized authority, but by the Spirit of the Lord. Life is greater than all the resources of material power.

Life in the Spirit

The Holy Spirit is emphatically both Giver and Lord of the life that is in Christ. "His action covers the whole life from first to last. He is the Spirit of Life for regeneration (John 3:5,8); the Spirit of Sonship for adoption (Rom. 8:15; Gal. 4:6); the Spirit of Holiness for sanctification (Rom. 8:5); the Spirit of Glory for transfiguration (2 Cor. 3:18; 1 Peter 4:14); and the Spirit of Promise for resurrection (Eph. 1:13; 4:30)." The believer is born of the Spirit, he believes in the Spirit, prays in the Spirit, and walks in the Spirit. From first to last he is sphered in the Presence of the Spirit and the Spirit dwells in him; just as in his natural life he lives in the air and the air dwells in him.

Delivered from the flesh, he lives in the Spirit. And what is the life in the Spirit? It is a life lived in the realm of the spiritual. It is a life in which there is no condemnation. Guilt is purged, sin is cleansed away, carnality is destroyed. There is not only an imputed righteousness by grace but a realized righteousness through faith. The things that bring condemnation have been put away, and life stands approved and accepted in the will of God. Instead of condemnation there is the assurance of Sonship and Heirship in Christ Jesus. One's life of prayer finds a new intelligence, intensity and power. The Spirit prays in the praying heart, and prayer in the Spirit prevails. Conquest takes the place of defeat, and the Spirit-filled life prevails in conflict as it prevails in prayer. Consequently there comes to the heart a deep sense of security in the love of God, and a Christlike compassion for the souls of the lost. The Spirit of Christ brings the mind of Christ, and baptizes us into the fellowship of His redeeming love. This is the abundant life Christ came to bring— the life filled with His Spirit.

The Law of the Spirit of Life

The Spirit is the Ruler, as well as the Giver of life. Rule means law, and there is a law of the Spirit of Life. There is no escape from law. There is a law of the flesh, a law of the mind, a law of sin, and a law of death. There is no escape from law in the life that is unregenerate. Neither is there any escape for those who live in the Spirit. It is another law, but it is still law. There is a law of faith, a law of grace, a law of truth, a law of life, and a law of the Spirit.

12

"The Spirit of Truth"

OUR LORD spoke of Himself as the Truth, and of the Holy Ghost as the Spirit of Truth. The revelation, inspiration, and interpretation of truth are in a special and unique sense the work of the Divine Spirit. God has spoken through His Spirit. It is reasonable to expect that He would. He had made man for fellowship, and it is incredible that God would expect fellowship without mutual speech, especially when the need of revelation became manifest. Had there been no sin, man would have still needed a guide to things beyond himself. Someone would have needed to tell him of things above and beyond himself, for there are many things that cannot be found by searching. By faith we know some of these things, but there is no sure basis for faith without revelation. Still more is revelation necessary when sin darkens the understanding. Love could not be silent in the presence of such need and peril. God has spoken. He has revealed His mind, declared His will, and set forth His way to Truth, and Life, and Power. By the Spirit of Truth God spoke through the prophets, and by Him has come the inspired and infallible revelation of God.

The Spirit and Revelation

By revelation is understood those truths made known by supernatural means, because they lie beyond the power of man to discover. Inspiration is concerned with the means and processes by which these truths are made known. Revelation comes by the Inspiration of the Spirit of Truth. It is in this way that we know anything authentic about creation and the events that happened before man was there to see. The records of these things must be either guesses or revealed truths. The same applies to all that we know of God in His nature and attributes, and still more of His redeeming purpose of love and grace. Man by searching cannot find God, but it has pleased God to make Himself known to the children of men. We know God by revelation, and in the knowledge of Him is the life which is life indeed. To revelation we owe also the knowledge of the final issues of the Kingdom of Grace. The ascended glory and the triumphant return of our glorious Lord are of such a character that no human mind could have conceived them. The sum of the divine revelation is in Jesus Christ the Son of God. Revealed truth is truth "as truth is in Jesus" (Eph. 4:21). He is the eternal Word of God; the oracle of God in human flesh. He is emphatically *the Truth*: the embodiment of Truth, the Word of Truth, and the sum of Truth. The eternal Word and the eternal Truth are one. The incarnate Word is the sum and substance of Truth. In Christ is God's final revelation of Truth, but in the Spirit of Truth is its unfolding, interpretation, and realization. It was the Spirit that made known the revelation, directed its development, and watched over its integrity.

The Bible is the record of the revelation of God through the Spirit. The prophets of the Old Testament claimed to be the spokesmen of God on the ground that they had received a revelation from God. They are God's messengers, for they have heard His voice. They gave account of the way the word of the Lord came to them, and their claim to speak for Him is that they have received His word. The same authority is claimed in the New Testament. The gospel came to the Apostles by revelation. Our Lord despaired of making them understand the glorious nature of His Cross, but He assured them that the Spirit of Truth would reveal it to them; and He did. Pentecost was the crowning day of revelation.

The Spirit and Inspiration

It was in this way the revelation came from God, and that is how the Scriptures came to be written. The revelation was before the record, and it was the revelation that created the necessity for the Scriptures. They are the work of the Spirit. Whatever may be the true theory of Inspiration, the Scriptures claim a special influence of the Spirit, by which they possess a divine quality and a final authority. They are inspired and infallible, and therefore the "divine rule of faith and conduct." There was given to inspired speakers and writers of the divine revelation a special and unique influence by which they were able faithfully to make known the truth revealed.

The Bible never defines Inspiration. It insists upon the fact, but it never attempts to explain the theory. That is left to the theologians, and the theory must be deduced from the facts, and it must take account of all the facts. For all practical purposes, the assurance that it is an energy of the Spirit of Truth, sufficient to secure accurate and adequate expression, satisfies all reasonable demands. The fault of most discussions on Inspiration is that they have overlooked some important facts and factors. Some have claimed for the Bible more than the Bible claims for itself, and others have ignored some of its demands. Both would have escaped their pitfalls if they had taken pains to know the doctrine of the Holy Spirit and understand the relation of the Spirit of Truth to the Word of God.

Modern methods have specialized in dissecting the Scriptures—and in nothing has the change wrought been so drastic and, for the time being, disastrous. It is claimed that the orthodox and traditional views have been demolished forever, and that never again will the Bible be regarded as a divine and infallible book. Great sport has been made of the superstitious reverence of the devout who accepted all its parts as equally inspired and of equal value. The so-called traditional view has been ignorantly or willfully misrepresented or flippantly caricatured. It is difficult to be patient with the specious shallowness and colossal vanity that masquerade under the claims of modernity and scientific criticism, but it will be plain in the end that they have helped to a better understanding of the truth. They have taught us much of the human and historical side of Inspiration. The Spirit works by human cooperation. He spoke "by the prophets." No prophecy came, as Weymouth translates it, of the prophets' own prompting. Holy men of God spoke as they were moved by the Holy Ghost. He moved; they spoke. There was no suspension of personal powers, personal consciousness, personal gifts. Inspiration intensified personality, but it neither changed nor confused it. The message was spoken by many voices, and when it came to be written, the writing of the Divine Word was by "a man's hand." A careful study of Luke 1:1–4, 1 Peter 1:11–12, 2 Peter 1:21, and Hebrews 1:1 would safeguard our thinking against many errors. There are diversities of Inspiration, but one Spirit, and He is the Spirit of Truth. There are sixty-six books in the Bible, but it is one Book. There are many writers, but only one Author. The unity of the progressive Word is the miracle of the Spirit in revealed truth.

The Spirit and Interpretation

Before man can see he must have sight and light. Eyes cannot see in the dark, and light shows nothing to the blind. So with regard to truth there must be the seeing eye and the illuminating light. The Word is Truth, but it is the Spirit of Truth that makes it the Living Word. Inspiration ceased within a hundred years after Christ's birth. The best writings of the second century reveal a transition that is an abrupt and abysmal gulf. Creative inspiration gave place to imitative devotion. The Holy Spirit was still in the Church, but He no longer inspired new revelations. "Since the New Testament times the Holy Spirit has illuminated truth, but has not revealed anything new."

All agree that we must have an interpreter. The Sacerdotalist holds that the Church is the custodian and interpreter of the Scriptures. He argues that the living voice is more than the written Word. That depends on whose voice it is. We do need an interpreter, an infallible teacher, a trustworthy guide, and the Interpreter of the inspired Word is the Spirit of Truth. The mere grammarian cannot find it. The controversialist cannot explain it. The critic knows not its secret. The carnal mind cannot perceive it. The natural man cannot possess it. The twice-born see. The anointed know. The Spirit that revealed illumines, and He that inspired interprets.

The Spirit of Truth honors the Word of Truth. He consents to be tried by the Word of God. Illuminations that come from Him are in harmony with the Word. He guides into all truth. The sons of God are led by the Spirit of Truth. The world cannot receive Him, but they know Him. In the world the Spirit of Truth convicts, challenges, condemns; to the Spirit-filled He illumines, interprets, and transforms.

Had a Scriptural view of the Person and work of the Holy Ghost been more powerfully prevalent in the Church, not merely in her formularies but in reality and life, there would never have been so much occasion given to represent the teaching of the Church on the inspiration of Scripture as "mechanical" and "converting men into automata"; and the whole question would not have assumed such a scholastic and metaphysical form. For then the living testimony and the written testimony would appear both as supernatural and Spirit-breathed. The more the supremacy of the Holy Ghost—divine, loving, and present—is acknowledged, the more the Bible is fixed in the heart and conscience. But if the "Book is viewed as the relic and substitute of a now absent and inactive Spirit, Bibliolatry and Bible-rejection are the necessary results." Without the Spirit of Truth even the Word of Truth is a dead letter. It is the Spirit that quickens, illumines, and interprets the Word.

The Spirit and Illumination

Jesus said: "Howbeit, when He the Spirit of Truth is come, He shall guide you into all the truth: for He shall not speak of Himself; but what things soever He shall hear, these shall He speak; and He shall declare unto you the things that are to come. He shall glorify Me: for He shall take of Mine, and shall declare it unto you" (John 16:13–14).

Divine truth is not of grammar, of learning, or of logic, but of the Holy Spirit of God. He is given to reveal "the deep things."

"The Spirit searcheth the deep things of God." There is no adjective in the Greek. It is not "deep things" but "deeps." There are fringes of the divine glory such as Moses and the prophets saw, and they are glorious and wonderful, but there are depths, abysses, like those of the heavens and the sea. Deep beyond deep, fathoms unfathomable, and these the Spirit of God searches and reveals. He does not search to discover. In Romans 8:27 and in Revelation 2:23 God and Christ are said to "search." It implies thoroughness, and not quest. The Spirit is ever active in fathoming the depths of God. His omniscience is ever exploring and revealing the depths of God. Romans 11:33 unites the ideas of depth and unsearchableness.

The point of the argument is that the deeps in God cannot be known by any other means than the revelation of the Holy Spirit. Just as the deep things in a man are known only to the spirit of a man, so the deeps of God are known only to and by the Spirit of God. Our wisdom cannot discover Him. The princes and rulers of the world's intellect and intelligence cannot know Him. The well is deep, and they have nothing wherewith to draw. The deep things are not discovered; they are received. They are not achieved; they are believed. They are not taught; they are revealed. The Spirit is the Spirit of God, and by Him we know the things of God.

The Spirit is given to glorify Christ. No man can know Jesus without the distinct revelation of the Spirit. The deeps of Christ cannot be explored by human wisdom. His life in Nazareth may be reconstructed by novelists, dramatized by genius, and immortalized by art; but the Christ is not in them. "No man can say that Jesus is the Lord, but by the Holy Ghost" (1 Cor. 12:3). The same is true of His teaching. Grammar cannot discover its truth, and the letter killeth. It is also true of His work. The Cross must always be an enigma, a stupidity, and anathema to the wisdom of this world. It belongs to the deeps known only to the Spirit and to those enlightened and instructed by Him. The depths of Christ are unsearchable. The love of Christ passeth knowledge. The grace of Christ is immeasurable. The glory of Christ is unfathomable. There are deeps beyond deep, heights beyond height. Deep calls unto deep, and glory unto glory. To the natural man they are without meaning; to the taught of the Spirit they are eternally sure. We know Him, and we know that we know Him because we have an anointing of the Holy One that takes of the things that are His and reveals them unto us.

The Renewal of the Mind

"The natural man receiveth not the things of the Spirit of God: for they are foolishness unto him; and he cannot know them because they are spiritually discerned." Part of the ministry of the Spirit of Truth, therefore, is the preparation and renewal of the mind of man for receiving the deep things of God. But who is sufficient to describe the transformation wrought by the Spirit in the consenting mind? The ancient Messianic prophecy finds fulfillment in the simplest believer.

> " The Spirit of the Lord shall rest upon Him,
>   The Spirit of wisdom and understanding,
>   The Spirit of counsel and might,
>   The Spirit of knowledge and of fear of the Lord."

But the Spirit's operation upon the mind does not end with the bestowal of understanding. The gift of the Spirit brings a sound mind as well as a new spirit. Both need to be renewed for the reception of truth as it is in Jesus (Eph. 4:21–23). The mind must be renewed, for through the renewed mind comes the transformed life and the proving of the will of God (Rom. 12:1–2). Dedication of the body as a living sacrifice must be sustained by the constant renewal of the mind. The Spirit of God dwells in the spirit of man to guide the mind into all truth. He interprets the mind of Christ, for He takes of the things of Christ and reveals them unto us. It is in this way the Spirit interpreted all things to our Lord. The Spirit worked through His mind. So the prophecy goes on:

> "And He shall be quick of understanding,
> And His delight shall be in the fear of the Lord;
> And He shall not judge after the sight of His eyes,
> Neither reprove after the hearing of His ears:
> But with righteousness shall He judge the poor,
> And reprove with equity for the meek of the earth."

And so the Christ is made unto us wisdom and righteousness and sanctification and redemption.

13

"The Spirit of Holiness"

THE TITLE of the Spirit most frequently used in the New Testament is the "Holy Spirit." The phrase "Spirit of Holiness" occurs but once, and it can hardly be claimed that it refers directly to the Holy Spirit. Paul says in Romans 1:4 that as Christ on the human side was of the seed of David, so on the divine side He was "declared to be the Son of God with power, according to the Spirit of Holiness, by the resurrection of the dead." It was not the Holy Spirit that the Apostle evidently had in mind, but our Lord's human spirit distinguished by holiness and conquering the powers of death. Elsewhere the resurrection of our Lord from the dead is attributed to the Holy Spirit; and even if it be the quality of our Lord's own spirit that made it "impossible that He should be holden of death," the human spirit was equipped, sanctified, and kept by the Divine Spirit. The phrase, however, reaches further than the resurrection, and implies that, by the Spirit of Holiness, men are sanctified in truth. His work is to glorify Christ and sanctify the saints, making holy the Body of Christ which is His Church.

What Is Holiness?

It is unfortunate that the term has ceased to attract even good people. There are many who regard it with suspicion, and some who dismiss it with scorn. It is not uncommon for it to be made the butt of cheap wit and the subject of some doubtful stories. This is all the more surprising because of the emphasis with which the New Testament insists upon its necessity, urges its experience, and enforces its obligations. There is little teaching and testimony on the subject, and, therefore, there is dense ignorance and much misundertanding. The subject is generally dismissed without inquiry, but even among those who take the trouble to think there is much misapprehension, and the reason is that due attention not given to the place and work of the Holy Spirit in the sanctification of the believer. He is the Sanctifier.

The meaning of holiness must be interpreted "according to the Scriptures." It has a Biblical content and value. It is no use to search for it in pagan literature, however classical, for the Biblical idea of holiness is not to be found elsewhere. Even in Israel it was of slow growth, and the idea passed through many stages before it took its complete and final form. Its root meaning is separation, and it was used of things dedicated to religious uses. Then God was conceived of as separate in majesty and apart in character, and holiness was ascribed to Him and His ways. This quality in God demanded a like quality in His people, and to His covenanted people He said, "Be ye holy, for I am holy." He chose them to be unto Him a holy people. For this purpose He called them out from among the nations. They were to be unto Him "a peculiar people" in whom all men should see a holy and sanctified personality. Holiness had its positive as well as its negative side. They were to be distinguished by moral and spiritual excellence as well as by ceremonial and national distinctions. Holiness is an experience as well as an attitude, a life as well as a separation. Their separation unto God was to be manifest in their likeness to Him. The supreme revelation and standard are in Jesus Christ. He revealed the Holy Father and made manifest the Holy Spirit, thereby making known in both God and man the Spirit of Holiness.

Believers are called unto holiness. "This is the will of God, even your sanctification." "God chose you from the beginning in sanctification of the Spirit." Without holiness grace fails in its purpose, and without it no man can see the Lord. The experience is set forth in various terms and under many forms, but in all its manifold representations the same root ideas persist and prevail. Holiness is an attitude of dedication and an experience of grace in which the heart is cleansed from sin and made perfect in love.

Misapprehensions About Holiness

There is a strange mistake abroad that holiness is something quite optional. It is regarded as desirable for certain people and in special circumstances, but its claims are by no means universal. There are preachers who sometimes speak of it as an alternative way to heaven, but as "all ways get there" the routes do not really matter. Holiness is regarded as an emotional luxury, if not as a spiritual fad. Its claims are deemed to be emotional rather than ethical, optional rather than imperative. There is little exposition of its character, and still less insistence upon its urgency; consequently, few seek to enter into the experience or take seriously the solemn words of Holy Scripture. Many take it for granted that if it is necessary it will come to them in due course without any concern of theirs. Such slackness accounts for much of the backsliding among believers. The Christian calling is one that demands "all diligence" and "earnest heed." Those who fail to seek after holiness "fall short of the grace of God," give opportunity to "the roots of bitterness to spring up," and become secular and worldly, like Esau, who bartered his spiritual inheritance for material good.

Another mistake made by many earnest Christians about holiness is that it comes by a gradual growth in grace and a steady progress of spiritual discipline. They are always growing towards it, but they never get into it—always struggling and striving to attain, but never entering into possession. The positive expectation is always seen to be afar off, and they die without having possessed. The hopeful future never becomes the positive now. The time never comes that calls for a definite step and a positive act of faith. But holiness does not come by growth; neither is it identified with growth. Growth is a process of life; holiness is the gift of abundant life. Growth is the result of health; holiness is health. Holiness implies a crisis, a new experience, a transformed life. It is not an achievement or an attainment, but a gift of grace in the Holy Ghost. It comes not by works but by faith.

Not a few good people mix up things that differ. They confuse cleansing with maturity, motive with achievement, love with blamelessness, and the perfection of grace with the perfection of the resurrection glory. People who ought to know blunder hopelessly over these things. Perhaps the confusion that is most common and most senseless is that which persists in associating perfection with finality. There are many people who seem to be afraid lest they should come to a point at which there will be no more room for improvement. They need not distress themselves, even their best friends being judges; but really such shallow and foolish thinking is without excuse. Love never exhausts its inheritance or reaches its limit in being made perfect. Health never hinders growth. The perfection of efficiency is surely not final but primary. No doctrine of the Bible has been stated with greater care, and if any man wills to possess he need not err as to the way.

Holiness Through the Spirit

The Scriptural method of sanctification is through the personal work of the Spirit of God. The law of the Spirit of life makes us free from the law of sin and death. It is God's work, wrought in the heart by the Holy Spirit who makes Christ our sanctification. There are diversities of operation in all the works of the Spirit, and the method of entering into possession is as manifold as the temperaments and conditions of human life. No two experiences are ever really alike. Generally there is an awakening of heart and mind in which there comes vision and persuasion. There is a conviction of need and a revelation of grace, a hunger and a search, a process and a crisis, an act of faith and an assurance of cleansing. It is as distinctly a second work of grace as regeneration is a new birth. Consecration is as practical as repentance, and sanctification as definite as regeneration. Unbelief stumbles at a name, and the heart shrinks from a crisis that involves a death and a resurrection. Satan multiplies difficulties, and an evil heart backs him. The way of life must be sought in the Holy Word and by the Holy Spirit, and the twofold guide will not fail those who seek with all their heart.

Holiness is in the spirit and of the Divine Spirit. It is not in forms and ordinances, not in "will worship and voluntary humility." It is not in prohibitions and self-denial. It is a spirit, a life, a principle, a dynamic. The Spirit of God indwells the spirit of man. He clothes Himself with man, and man is clothed in the presence and power of the Spirit. The body is the temple of the Spirit. Christ lives in men through the Spirit. He is no longer a model but a living Presence. Christian faith does not copy Him; it lives Him. Christ is not imitated, but reproduced. Life is sanctified because He possesses it, lives it, transforms it. The Spirit of God does not work upon us; He *lives* in us. This is the contrast between the *works* of the flesh and the *fruit* of the Spirit. Works are by the sweat of man's brow; fruit is God's gift to man. Fruit does not come by toil but by appropriation, assimilation, and abiding. Holiness makes life fruitful because it abides in the Living Word and gives free scope to the Spirit of Life. The Spirit of Holiness makes the heart clean, the mind true, the faculties fit, and the life fruitful—by making His holiness ours.

14

"The Spirit of Love"

LOVE is the last word in religion. It completes the revelation of God and sums up the whole duty of man. Love is of God, and the Spirit of God is the "Spirit of Love." This designation of the Spirit is not so well known as some others, but is the quality that gives value to all the rest.

The Love of the Spirit

There is one passage that speaks directly of the love of the Spirit. "Now I beseech you, brethren, by our Lord Jesus Christ, and by the love of the Spirit, that ye strive together with me in your prayers to God for me" (Rom. 15:30). There is some dispute as to whether the love of the Spirit refers to the love which the Spirit produces in us or to the personal love of the Spirit for us. The former meaning finds considerable favor, and in that case the Apostle would mean: "I beseech you, brethren, by our Lord Jesus Christ, and the love of your spirit to me, that ye strive together with me in your prayers." Such a request would be natural enough, but the form of the request would be unnatural and strange. The phrase becomes awkward and enigmatical if it is intended to mean the love which the Spirit gives, but it is natural and plain if it names the Son and the Spirit as the ground of appeal. The entreaty names all the Persons of the Trinity, and beseeches "for the Lord Jesus Christ's sake, and by the love of the Spirit whom He hath given to us," that they will pray with him and for him. The love of the Spirit is the emotion and quality of love in the Spirit; it is His love, not ours, that is the basis of appeal.

This is the unmistakable teaching of the Word. Romans 5:5 speaks of the love of God that has been shed in our hearts by the Holy Ghost being given unto us. This must mean that it is God's own love that is shed in our hearts. It is a quality of life that is given to us, and this quality comes from and through the Holy Ghost. It is not a gift that can be received apart from the Giver. The love comes with the Spirit.

Love stands first in the order of fruit. Dr. Campbell Morgan argues that it is the whole fruit, and that all the rest of the list in Galatians 5:22–23 are but manifestations of the one great and all-inclusive quality of love. Be that as it may, and it may well be so, there can be no doubt that love in the believer is the fruit of the love of the Spirit. Fruit is an expression of life, and love is the fruit of the Spirit. The fruit is not of our growth. It is the result of abiding in Christ by the Spirit of Love dwelling in us. Love is the first, the chief, the most notable result when the Spirit of Love dwells in us.

There is another notable passage which speaks of

the believer's "love in the Spirit" (Col. 1:8). This is something more than "spiritual love." It means that our love of the brethren is a love not human in its origin; not mere good nature and goodwill perfected by grace, but the love of God that dwells in our hearts by the good Spirit of Love. "For God hath not given us the spirit of fear, but [the Spirit] of power, of love, and of a sound mind" (2 Tim. 1:7). The Spirit of God is not a spirit of fear, or a spirit of bondage, but the Spirit of Adoption, the Spirit of Truth, the Spirit of Power, and the Spirit of Love. Just as His coming into the heart brings assurance, and truth, and power, so it brings the conscious possession of love shed abroad in the heart, and the love with which we love God is God's own love imparted to us, and implanted in us by the Holy Ghost, the Spirit of Love.

The Ministry of Love

The ministry of the Spirit is a ministry of love. The Church of Christ has chosen to call Him the Comforter. The ministry of consolation may be a very small part of the meaning of "Paraclete," but the human heart will never give up the name "Comforter" for that of "Advocate." "The comfort of the Holy Ghost" is treasured as a priceless possession more precious than power; more even than truth. Sorrow is more universal than the thirst for knowledge, and in the day of distress consolation is more than might. The word "Paraclete" means more than Comforter, but in meaning more it cannot mean less. The Comforter is in the Paraclete. Our Lord promised that He would save His disciples from the desolation of orphans. He even declared that they would gain by the exchange of His presence for that of the Paraclete. "It is expedient for you that I go away: for if I go not away, the Comforter will not come unto you; but if I go, I will send Him unto you" (John 16:7). Even so, it is hard to see how He could expect them to be comforted by the promise of One who would more than fill His place. Fancy a dying mother making any such promise to her children. They would protest that they did not believe any such gain possible; that they did not want anyone better, for to them none could be half so good. Our Lord said it, however, and none dared to deny it or even challenge His words.

The Spirit came to fulfill our Lord's ministry of love in the world. The world cannot receive Him, for the Spirit of Love cannot dwell in a heart of hate or a spirit of worldliness. The world does not even know Him. In this He shares the fate of the Son—and in His succession He takes up the redemptive work of Jesus Christ, the Saviour of the world. He seeks the lost. With loving patience He pursues and pleads. It is He who convicts the world. The sacrifice of Calvary is perpetuated in the Spirit of Love. Like our Lord, He suffers the contradiction of sinners against themselves. Love agonizes where it is powerless to help. What anguish is there like love in despair? The mother who has to stand helpless and see her child perish goes mad with grief. The father who strives in vain to keep his boy from the madness of folly either turns gray or grows hard. Think of the grief of the Spirit of Love! Who can measure the anguish of His rebuffs, reproaches, and rejection. Love is sensitive. It shrinks from distrust, indifference and reproach. It yearns for love. So the Spirit yearns for us "even unto jealous envy" (James 4:5, R.V., margin).

There is the same sensitive love in all His work. The love of God in Christ made Him the friend of sinners. He associated with them. His enemies said He was a chum with them. He sat at meat with them, and was evidently welcome among them. It does not seem to occur to us what contact with sin must have cost Him. Love shrinks from the ugly and offensive, but it overcomes and loves all the more for the greater need. The Spirit of God dwells now in men's hearts. When Christ came a body was prepared for Him; it had the limitations of humanity, but it was without sin. The present temple of the Holy Ghost is not thus prepared for His coming. He comes to hearts confessedly unclean. The heart is deceitful above all things and desperately wicked, and yet He comes to abide at its very seat and center. Through what travail the Spirit of Love must pass before the heart becomes indeed His temple and His home. The patience of the Spirit would be impossible were it not for His love.

The Perfecting of Love

"Herein is love made perfect with us." Wherein? In the secret of the indwelling Spirit of Love.

"Hereby know we that we abide in Him, and He in us, because He hath given us of His Spirit."

"God is love; and he that abideth in love abideth in God, and God abideth in him."

"Herein is love made perfect with us, that we may have boldness in the day of judgment; because as He is, even so are we in this world. There is no fear in love: but perfect love casteth out fear, because fear hath punishment; and he that feareth is not made perfect in love" (1 John 4:13,16, 17–18).

The whole secret is in the "Hereby" and "Herein." Perfect love is by the Spirit of Love. There are two senses in which love may be in need of perfecting. It may be defective in quality or it may be deficient in quantity. If the love shed abroad in the heart is the very love of God Himself, it cannot be defective in quality, but it may be deficient in range and scope of operation. The Spirit fills what is given. He does not wait for fullness of knowledge in us. Wherever there is a sincere purpose to serve Christ He accepts the motive, however great the ignorance. There is a law of the Spirit of Life, and it patiently waits through all the stages of the blade, the ear, and the full corn in the ear. He yearns for fullness of love, and as He led to repentance so He leads to surrender and fullness of blessing. Love is made perfect when the Spirit of Love alone reigns in all the heart and life. We love because the Spirit of Love dwells in us, and that love is made perfect when the indwelling Trinity of Love permeates, dominates, and possesses us entirely to the praise of His glory and the excellence of His power.

15

"The Spirit of Fire"

"**O**UR GOD is a consuming fire." The elect symbol of His presence is fire—a blaze unlike any kindled on earth—and the chosen sign of His approval is the sacred flame. Covenant and sacrifice, sanctuary and dispensation were sanctified and approved by the descent of fire. "The God that answereth by fire, He is God." That is the final universal test of deity. Jesus Christ came to bring fire upon the earth. The symbol of Christianity is not a cross but a tongue of fire.

"Strange Fire"

So universally is this recognized that men substitute unauthorized fire for the fire of God. A fireless altar is the sign of desertion and death. It means that the temple has lost its God and worship has died out in the land. There must be fire or there can be no religion. If it cannot be procured from heaven it must be kindled by earthly means. There is much speculation about the "strange fire" offered with such terrible results by the sons of Aaron. The offense for which they died is expressed in the words "they offered fire which the Lord had not commanded" (Lev. 10:1). The exact form of their sin is not stated, but the reasonable explanation is that they carried into their ministry unconsecrated fire. It did not come from the altar. The precise form of this transgression is no longer possible, but the sin is common to all ages. It is a kind of will-worship, by which man substitutes his own enthusiasms for the will of God. God's revealed will is ignored and the divine commandment set aside for other ways and means in worship and service.

Earth fires can soon be set ablaze. It is so much easier to excite the passion than to kindle souls. Thorns crackle as they burn, and the flying sparks arrest and amuse. True, the fuel is soon exhausted and the fire fizzles out, but they serve while they last.

The penalty for unholy fire in the sanctuary is death. "Behold, all ye that kindle a fire, that gird yourselves about with firebrands: walk ye in the flame of your fire, and among the brands that ye have kindled. This shall ye have of mine hand; ye shall lie down in sorrow." Earth-kindled fires burn fiercely, but they burn out. They allure to deeper darkness. Lights that glare and dazzle blind the eyes. Artificial excitement destroys spiritual sensibility. Satiated desire fails. When religion turns to humanity for its inspiration and to the world for its power, God is dethroned and the sanctuary becomes a secularized fellowship.

Stage Fire

Strange fire may be offered in sincerity and in good

faith. Stage fire is a trick. In the absence of the supernatural, earnest souls may turn to the best substitutes they can find and believe they are doing God's service. When the fires of spiritual devotion go out, ritualism finds its opportunity. Aids to voluptuous meditation take the place of reverent adoration. If there be no power to cast out demons, transform sinners and save souls, there are other ministries within reach. John did no miracle; may not a ministry of "water baptism" avail for our day and generation? If we have no fire from on high by which men's souls can be saved, there are minds to be instructed and bodies to be fed. Churches destitute of divine fire may devote themselves fervently to good works, but stage fire is a mockery and a pretense. Stage lights have found their way into the Church. The red glare dazzles, but it does not burn. Fireworks are brilliant, but they end with the hour. No ideals are kindled, no ministry impelled, no sacrifice inspired. The pretense of spirituality is the worst profanity. Strange fire is less offensive than stage fire. A religion of mere emotion and sensationalism is the most terrible of all curses that can come upon any people. The absence of reality is sad enough, but the aggravation of pretense is a deadly sin.

Holy Ghost Fire

What is the fire of the Holy Ghost? Everywhere earnest believers are lamenting its absence and praying for a Pentecost of fire.

What is this fire? The Scriptures evidently regard it as the supreme need of the Church and the final gift of God. The prophets associated it with the Messiah, and promised it as the unique triumph of His coming. It marked the difference between the old dispensation and the new. John's ministry shook the nation but was only preparatory. "I indeed baptize with water; . . . He shall baptize you with the Holy Ghost and with fire." Our Lord spoke of the coming of fire as the one purpose of His mission and the fruit of His sufferings and death. "I came," He says, "to cast fire on the earth." The supreme need of the Church is fire. The one persistent prayer of them that "sigh and cry" is for the fiery baptism of Pentecost. What do we mean by fire? When Jesus promised the gift of fire, what did He mean them to expect? In our impassioned pleading for the descent of fire, what is it we want? For what does this elect symbol stand? Our God is a consuming fire; the gift of the Holy Ghost is a baptism of fire; Christianity is a religion of fire; we are saved by fire. If fire is so vital and comprehensive, it is important its meaning should be clearly understood.

Moral and Spiritual Passion

Whatever this fire may be, it is identified with the Person of the Holy Ghost. The Baptism of the Spirit is the baptism of fire. Our Lord's straitening for the baptism of blood was followed by the fullness of Pentecost in the gift of the Spirit of Fire. Its power was moral and spiritual. Men's souls were charged, saturated, enveloped, in the Spirit of God. The divine life entered into them. The passion of God possessed them with the intensity of fire. His love was shed

abroad in their hearts, and His holiness became the
master passion of their souls. They burned and they
shone: burning and shining lights. They were intense
as they were breezy, fiery as they were jubilant,
impassioned as they were daring. The spirit of cold
obedience was kindled into an enthusiasm for
righteousness, and the slavish sense of duty burst into
a flame of eager devotion. That is the miracle of
Pentecost. It kindles the fires of Christ's soul in the
souls of men. They receive, realize, and reproduce His
mind, His heart, His life. His zeal becomes the all-
pervasive character of their lives. They manifest His
fervent devotion to the will of the Father, His holy
passion for reality and righteousness, His consuming
zeal for the salvation of the lost. It kindles a fervent
devotion to God, a passion for righteousness, and a
consuming desire to seek and save the lost. Religion
at flame-heat illumines the mind, energizes every
faculty, and impassions every element of compassion.
Fire does not mean rant, or noise, or ruthless self-will.
It acts differently on different material and in different
people, but in all it burns, kindles, and glows. It is
religion at white-heat.

The Offense of Fire in Religion

Fire in religion awakens a peculiar sense of distrust
in the modern mind. There is no objection to it
anywhere else. Enthusiasm in politics and recreation,
fervor in reform and business, intensity in work and
friendship, are among the most coveted qualities of
modern life. In religion they are bad form. Enthusiasts

in piety are suspect. Christians full of zeal are merely tolerated where they are not despised. They are regarded as intellectually inferior—the "babes and sucklings" to whom God has no other way of revealing things precious to the soul. Their conception of religion is "narrow and antiquated" and their experience of it "too emotional and fervid." It is sometimes said they are defective in ethical balance and moral stamina, and they lack the charity which appreciates other types of goodness. Judged in the lump, the saints of the fire-heart are condemned as unlovely, undesirable, and unreasonable.

For things not fireproof, burning is not a pleasant sensation; but then, only that which can "dwell in everlasting burning" can be saved. We are saved by fire. Light is not enough, and water is not enough. Knowledge does not save, neither is cleanliness the equivalent of grace. Salvation is of the heart. External conventionality and correct observance may make a Pharisee, but never a Christian. It is by a holy passion kindled in the soul that we live the life of God. Truth without enthusiasm, morality without emotion, ritual without soul, are the things Christ unsparingly condemned. Destitute of fire they are nothing more than a godless philosophy, an ethical system, and a superstition. Moral and spiritual passion are of the essence of the religion of Christ.

The Power of Fire

The penalty of intensity may be narrowness but its reward is power. It submits all things to a severe test, and what will not assimilate it mercilessly assails. Fire cannot compromise. The logic of passion is direct, simple, relentless. Cool calculation is impossible to men ablaze. Inspiration despises dissimulation. Issues are simple when the heart is intense. The pure flame of a holy enthusiasm is a safer guide than the dry light of cold reason. The soul's safety is in its heat. Fire is the best defense against corruption. If we would be safe we must be clothed with zeal as with a garment. Our religion is only secure when it is guarded by "a wall of fire round about."

It is fire that prevails. For fifty days the facts of the gospel were complete, but no conversions were recorded. Pentecost registered three thousand souls. It is the cause that sets men ablaze that wins converts. Gladstone's fiery passion routed Parliaments and slew the giants of oppression. Wesley, Whitefield, and General Booth wrought wonders by the fire kindled of the Holy Ghost. Men ablaze are invincible. Hell trembles when men kindle. Sin, worldliness, unbelief, hell, are proof against everything but fire. The Church is powerless without the fire of the Holy Ghost. Destitute of fire, nothing else counts; possessing fire, nothing else really matters. The one vital need is fire. How we may receive it, where we may find it, by what means we may retain it, are the most vital and urgent questions of our time. One thing we know: it comes only with the presence of the Spirit of God, Himself the Spirit of Fire. God alone can send the fire. It is His Pentecostal gift.

16

The Fruit of the Spirit

THERE ARE nine gifts of the Spirit and nine graces of the Spirit. The graces of the Spirit are love, joy, peace, longsuffering, gentleness, goodness, faithfulness, meekness, temperance. The Scriptures never confuse gifts and graces. Gifts are for service, and are bestowed in the sovereign wisdom of the Spirit. They are given according to natural endowment as the talents were— according to the ability of those who received them. They are given according to grace: "Having then gifts differing according to the grace that is given to us." The differing gifts are adapted to the kind of service to which by the grace of God we are called, whether of prophecy, ministry, teaching, exhortation, beneficence, administration, or works of mercy. Each may have some gift, some may have more than one; but all gifts of the Spirit are according to the election of grace and are given for the effective working, by each, of the divine will. They are also according to faith. There is a faith that is among the gifts of the Spirit, but there is a faith also that is basic to all gifts, and "God hath dealt to every man the measure of faith."

Fruit Not Gifts

The graces of the Spirit are the fruit of the Spirit.

There are three leading passages that speak of the Christian character as fruit. The first is our Lord's allegory of the Vine and the Branches; the second is St. Paul's catalog of nine virtues which he calls "the fruit of the Spirit"; and the third is Peter's list of Christian graces which he regards as the fruitful result of the life of Christ in the soul. There are many other passages in which the figure of fruit is used, but in these three representative passages there is set forth the conditions of fruitfulness, the cluster of fruit, and the process of fruitage. In the figure of the Vine the Holy Spirit is not mentioned, but in Christ's comparing Himself to a vine and His disciples to its branches, the plant corresponds to His extended Body and its life to His Spirit. The diffusion of life is the work of the Holy Ghost, and the fruit by which the Father is glorified is the fruit of the Spirit. Apart from Christ there is neither life nor fruit, and without the Spirit of Christ there can be neither union nor abiding.

Our Lord does not identify the specific fruit. What He emphasizes is the fact that it *is* fruit, and that it is fruit directly from *Himself.* Some have "no fruit," and they are cast forth as a branch that is withered; others are described as having "fruit," "more fruit," "much fruit," and "fruit that abides." The conditions of fruitfulness are union with Christ, being purged or cleansed by the Father, abiding in Christ and having Christ abiding in us. St. Paul sums up all this teaching of the Vine and its Branches in the phrase "the fruit of the Spirit." He enlarges upon neither conditions nor process, for everything is implied in the word *fruit*. He assumes both conditions and process and sets forth the result. This explains the difference between his list and Peter's. Paul begins where Peter ends. One gives the result, the other dwells on the process of cultivation. Peter begins at conversion, by which the soul has "escaped"; enlarging on this experience of deliverance he says, "Yea, and for this very cause adding on your part all diligence, in your faith supply virtue; and in your virtue knowledge; and in your knowledge temperance; and in your temperance patience; and in your patience godliness; and in your godliness love of the brethren; and in your love of the brethren love" (2 Pet. 1:5–7, R.V.). The process begins in faith and ends in love. Then the Apostle Paul takes up the list: "The fruit of the Spirit is love, joy, peace, longsuffering, kindness, goodness, faithfulness, meekness, temperance" (Gal. 5:22–23).

Garden or Factory

In the Galatians passage the fruit of the Spirit is placed in contrast with the works of the flesh; and a striking contrast they make. The catalog of sinful works begins with the sins of the flesh and passes on to idolatry, discord, and drunkenness. The fruit of the Spirit begins with the characteristics of the spiritual mind and passes on to its manifestation in personal character, social virtues, and practical conduct. The most striking feature of the contrast is the emphatic change from works to fruit. Works belong to the workshop; fruit belongs to the garden. One comes from the ingenuity of the factory; the other is the silent growth of abounding life. The factory operates with dead stuff; the garden cultivates living forces to their appointed end. Works are always in the realm of dead things: every building is built out of dead material. The tree must die before it can be of use to the builder. There is no life in stones and brick, in steel joists and iron girders. They are all dead and in the process of disintegration. Nothing material lasts. Man's best works fail and fade, crumble and pass away. "The works of the flesh are these"—these are the products of all the operations of the flesh. The sinner becomes a victim of devilish ingenuity and cunning—a monotonous machine from which are turned out "fornication, uncleanness, lasciviousness, idolatry, sorcery, enmities, strife, jealousies, wraths, factions, divisions, heresies, envying, drunkenness, revellings, and such like." That is the factory that keeps up the supply of the devil's kingdom and furnishes hell with the souls of the damned.

Fruit does not come from man's labor. It requires his diligence, but it is neither his invention nor his product. He does not make the flowers. No skill of his brings the golden harvest of the fields or the luscious fruit upon the trees. When man has done all he can, then God begins and life proceeds. Fruit is God's work. The phrase "fruit of the Spirit" assigns the graces of the Christian character to their proper source. They are not of man's producing. They do not spring from the soil of the carnal nature. Men do not gather grapes of thorns, or figs of thistles. Every tree brings forth fruit after its kind. The fruit of the Vine is not deposited in its branches to be quickened by an act of faith. It grows by the life that is in the Vine. Salvation is by grace, and the Christian virtues are the fruit of the indwelling presence of the Spirit of Life. Fruit, not works!

The Cultivation of Fruit

Fruit implies cultivation. "My Father is the husbandman." A neglected garden grows weeds in plenty, but its fruitfulness soon passes away. The gardener is a busy man. He has to be always caring for the things he grows. They only respond to love; they need protection, nourishment, and cleansing. Pruning is the surgery of love. "My Father is the Gardener." He holds the knife. Chastening is proof of love. For the present it may not be joyous, but grievous. The present pruning is for future perfecting. It is often a painful process, but the glory of the Father is in the yield of the life in its fruit of the Spirit. Fruit must not be confused with gifts any more than it must be mistaken for works. Such confusion often leads to doubt and distress. It is not an uncommon thing for earnest workers in the Church to imagine that if they are filled with the Spirit they will be endowed with marvelous and miraculous power for service. Examples have been quoted of wonderful enduement that has turned commonplace men into marvels of power, and they look for like results. Gifts, however, are not fruit. They may exist apart from great spirituality. The Corinthians were rich in gifts and poor in fruit. Our

Lord told of some who wrought wonders in His name, but they were none of His. Fruit is for all; His gifts He gives to each severally as He will. The fruit of the Spirit consists of sanctified dispositions. Gifts are according to the basis of natural endowment; fruit is the perfecting of grace in heart and life. Gifts apart from fruit do not glorify Him. To glory in gifts bringeth a snare, but fruit is sacrificial and sacramental and brings glory to all. It grows by abiding, and is perfected without noise or fuss, without anxiety or care. God glories in fruit.

The Nine Graces

The term "fruit" is singular, and though the declared number is plural, the grammar is correct. There is no grammatical difficulty any more than in the statement that "the wages of sin is death." The term is generic, and is used of the graces that follow as we use it of a cluster of grapes. They refer to character, and set forth the kind of man the Spirit produces rather than the things He inspires him to do. The nine elements have been divided into three sections of three each. (1) In relation to God: love, joy, peace. (2) In relation to our fellows: longsuffering, gentleness, goodness. (3) In relation to ourselves: faithfulness (not faith), meekness, self-control. Perhaps all such divisions are a little arbitrary. It is much more likely that the singular term was meant to indicate unity, and all the nine belong to all three divisions.

In newspaper English, the passage would read something like this: The Fruit of the Spirit is an affectionate, lovable disposition, a radiant spirit and a cheerful temper, a tranquil mind and a quiet manner, a forbearing patience in provoking circumstances and with trying people, a sympathetic insight and tactful helpfulness, generous judgment and a big-souled charity, loyalty and reliableness under all circumstances, humility that forgets self in the joy of others, in all things self-mastered and self-controlled, which is the final mark of perfecting.

This is the kind of character that is the fruit of the Spirit. Everything is in the word "fruit." It is produced not by striving but by abiding, not by worrying but by trusting, not by works but by faith.

If this is the fruit of the Spirit, for whom is the fruit grown?

17

The Gifts of the Spirit

THE HOLY SPIRIT is Himself a Gift. In the Gift of the Spirit there are gifts. "Wherefore He saith, When He ascended up on high, He led captivity captive, and gave gifts unto men . . . and He gave some to be apostles; and some, prophets; and some, evangelists; and some, pastors and teachers; for the perfecting of the saints, for the work of ministering, unto the building up of the Body of Christ" (Eph. 4:8–12). "Now there are diversities of gifts, but the same Spirit. And there are diversities of administration, but the same Lord. And there are diversities of operations, but it is the same God which worketh all in all. But the manifestation of the Spirit is given to every man to profit withal" (1 Cor. 12:4–7).

Diversities of Manifestation

The manifestation of the Spirit is not always the same. There are diversities of gifts, differences of administration, operation, and manifestation, but the same Spirit. There is a manifold variety of the one

Spirit. There are varieties according to temperament, according to capability, according to grace, and according to function. The failure to remember this ensnares the unwary. They look for the experiences and gifts in others to be given to them. To some it is given to be as men filled with new wine, to others it is given to speak with tongues, and to others to work miracles of healing and of power—and we are apt to think these are invariable and inseparable from the Holy Spirit baptism and fullness. The Spirit divides to every man severally as He wills, but the gifts of the Spirit are no more arbitrary than the elections of grace. In the distribution of the talents each received "according to his several ability." Spiritual gifts must not be interpreted as natural endowments, but the principle of distribution is the same and two are not unrelated. The gifts of the Spirit transcend the gifts of nature, but they function through the sanctified powers of man. There is a new creation, but it is along the lines of natural endowment. Not all have the same gifts, and one deciding factor in the will of the Spirit is according to the ability of sanctified nature to receive and function. The scope is not according to our natural talents but "according to the power that worketh in us," and the power works consistent with personality. The natural man cannot receive the things of the Spirit, but it is to spiritual men spiritual gifts are given according to each man's individual ability in the will of the Spirit.

"All have not the gift of healing, neither do all speak with tongues." Neither does the Baptism of the Spirit make all evangelists. This is a snare into which many fall. They read of the mighty Pentecostal experience of evangelists who have won souls for Christ by the thousand. The evangelist links soul-converting power with the gift of the Spirit of Power, and it is almost impossible to separate the two. Therefore as it worked in them it may be expected to work in us, and many have passed through agonies of disillusionment and disappointment. God does not make every Spirit-filled man a Moody, a William Booth, a Thomas Cook, or a Thomas Champness. He gives the Spirit to some that they may be ministers of helpfulness; to some that they may be faithful witnesses; and to others that they may be sanctified mothers who are keepers at home and miracles of patience, wisdom, and sweetness. To each there is a gift of the Spirit, and whatever the kind of gift, there is to all the gift of power for effective service and testimony. Each receives power. Pentecost swallows up ineffectiveness in power and banishes fear in the victory of courageous faith.

Distinctiveness of Gifts

The gifts of the Spirit are distinct from natural talents and from the fruit of the Spirit. They are related to both and distinct from both. The fullness of the Spirit vitalizes natural powers, quickens dormant faculties, and reinforces capabilities. Fire quickens, energizes, clarifies. The brain gets a new quality of alertness, endurance and effectiveness. The mind receives new powers of perception, intelligence and understanding. The heart finds a new clarity of vision, a new simplicity of motive, and a new intensity of emotion. The impossible becomes capable of achievement in the sanctified powers of the natural man. These are undoubtedly the work of the Spirit, but the gifts of the Spirit are distinct from these, and they transcend the powers of even sanctified natural powers. They are not unrelated, and yet they are in some ways independent. There are nine gifts of the Spirit: wisdom, knowledge, faith, miracles, healing, prophecy, discernment of spirits, tongues, interpretation of tongues.

Wisdom and knowledge are related to intelligence and learning, and yet they are so distinct that they are undiscoverable from the natural powers of man, and are given to those who have neither natural sagacity nor education.

Faith is man's sixth sense. We live by faith. We walk by faith. We do everything by faith. The gift of the Spirit is faith. By the Spirit faith sees the Invisible and proves the reality of the unrealized.

Healing is a gift of the Spirit. This is not the same as the sanctified skill of medical science. Those to whom it was given in the Early Church knew little or nothing of medicine. The sick were instructed to send, not for the doctors, but the elders, and the appointed means of healing were anointing and the prayer of faith. None could heal indiscriminately. Paul kept Luke, the beloved physician, with him in his journeys, and Trophimus was left at Miletus, sick. The Lord the Healer still gives to men the gift of healing by His Spirit; and the gift works quite apart from medical knowledge or the use of drugs or herbs.

Miracles are the gift of the Spirit, and the age of

miracles is not past.

Prophecy is more than insight or foresight, though the prophet is both a seer and a forth-teller.

By the gift of the Spirit there is a God-given discernment of spirits. The Apostles had it. Many prophets of God also had it.

The gifts of tongues and their interpretation come last on the list—and are first in controversy. There is a gift of tongues that is given for a sign, and there is a gift of tongues that is for the perfecting of the saints and the building up of the Body of Christ. It means more than a gift for acquiring an unknown language, and it is certainly no substitute for such learning. A careful study of the New Testament places this gift last among the enduements of the Church and specially safeguards it against abuse.

All the gifts of the Spirit give a supernatural power to the work of sanctified natural endowments—so that men are challenged to see and consider cause and effect and thus find there is nothing in the natural man to account for what is manifestly of God.

The Relation of Fruit and Gifts

Fruit and gifts are not identical. Fruit belongs to character; gifts are enduements of power. Gifts are an evidence of the Spirit; but they are no proof of holiness. Gifts are according to the elections of the sovereign will of the Spirit of God; fruit is the manifestation of cultivated life. Gifts are for service; fruit is for character. Gifts are functional; fruit is a quality of life. Gifts are bestowed; fruit is a manifestation. Gifts may be given immediately and complete; fruit is implanted and of gradual development. They are both of the Spirit and are intimately connected with one another, but they are not inseparable, much less identical. The gifts of the Spirit are given to people who are elect according to the sovereign will of God, who by His Spirit divides to each one individually as He wills. Love, in which is included all the fruit, is not in the list of spiritual gifts. Fruit is for all; gifts are for those for whom they have been prepared. All may not prophesy, but all must love. We may covet gifts, but we must bear fruit. Gifts cannot take the place of fruit.

The Function of Spiritual Gifts

"Having then gifts differing according to the grace that is given to us, whether prophecy, let us prophesy according to the proportion of our faith; or ministry, let us give ourselves to our ministry; or he that teacheth, to his teaching; or he that exhorteth, to his exhorting; he that giveth, let him do it with liberality; he that ruleth, with diligence; he that showeth mercy, with cheerfulness" (Rom. 12:6–8, R.V.). The gifts of the Spirit are for service, and they differ according to the kind of ministry to be fulfilled. Occasion may determine function. There are seasons when special gifts abound. Some are permanent. Others are given for special vocations and exceptional occasions; as, for example, the gifts that came upon Timothy by the laying on of hands, and the special manifestations of power in times of special visitation. There are no reasons why the gifts of the Spirit should be operative in one dispensation and not in another. They did not cease at the close of the Apostolic Age. They have been manifest in all ages of the Church, and there are abundant proofs that they are still available to the faith and need of the Church. There is no reason why they should not be more manifest, and perhaps there is a greater need for them now than in some other times. The wonders of man rival the miracle of God. The psychic is hardly distinguishable from the spiritual. The Dragon-Lamb (Rev. 13:11–14) is capable of great signs. In the realms of wisdom and knowledge, faith and healing, miracles of power, prophecies and discernment of the occult, tongues and their inter- pretation, the wisdom of this world outvies the works of modern religion. The counterfeit outbids the true, but the true is the power that destroys the false. A revival of spiritual gifts in the Church would bring to naught the mocking pretensions of the world. Pagan cannot cast out pagan, any more than Satan can cast out Satan, but in the Spirit of God there is victory over the world.

Safeguards Against Abuse

Gifts are liable to abuse. In the Early Church they appealed to unspiritual men who desired them for carnal purposes and thought they had a commercial value. They are still commercialized, though not always for their cash value. In the Corinthian church they became a fruitful source of rivalry, jealousy and disorder. Those possessed of one gift claimed priority in importance and precedence in order. The root of the difficulty lay in the fact that carnal people were in possession of spiritual gifts and used them for carnal ends. Spiritual gifts are no proof of spirituality. The New Testament nowhere makes spiritual gifts the sign of holiness, and there were some greatly endowed of whom Jesus said that at the last it would be declared that He never knew them. There is no suggestion that the gifts were not genuine, but they were perverted to wrong ends or exercised in the wrong spirit. This is a serious difficulty to many, but the Scriptures make it plain that in a church that "came behind in no gift, waiting for the coming of the Lord," there were carnalities that would have disgraced a decent pagan assembly. Gifts are not substitutes for grace, and ignorance and carnality have made them a menace to holiness of heart and integrity of character.

The safeguards against abuse are in the loyalties of faith. The first is loyalty to the lordship of Christ. That is the first law of Christian discipleship and the continual standard of Christian life and service. The second line of defense is loyalty to the Word of God. The Word and the Spirit are never at variance, for the Word of Truth attests the Spirit of Truth, and the Spirit interprets, corroborates, verifies, and confirms the Word. No wisdom is of God that is not according to the Scriptures. There is also laid down a practical rule of loyalty to fellowship in the Body of Christ. Edification is the test and order is the rule. The gifts of prophecy and tongues came into competition, and for these gifts definite rules were laid down, but the law of love applied to all.

18

The Law of the Spirit

THERE is no escape from law. Grace, love, and faith are all declared to be the end of law, but they are also subject to law. There is a law of grace, a law of love, a law of faith, and a law of the Spirit of Life. The Christian set free from the law of sin and death is still under law. He exchanges one kingdom for another, but in each there is law. Salvation, which is of grace and not of works, brings deliverance from the law of works, but it subjects the believer to the law of grace and truth.

Consider Paul: Paul glories above all others in his liberty through grace. The law has no more authority over him. Whether he conforms to it or rejects it is a thing of no account to him. Even so, though free, he brings himself under bondage to all, that he might gain some. To the Jews he became as a Jew, that he might gain the Jews; to them that were under the law, as under the law (not being himself under law) that he might gain them that were under the law; to them that were without law, as without law, that he might gain them that were without law. His argument is familiar, and his authority and example are often

quoted in defense of diplomacy, expediency, and tact;
but there is a vital clause in the argument that is often
omitted. The Apostle's freedom was not lawless. All
his expediency was subject to law: "Not being without
law to God, but under law to Christ" (1 Cor. 9:20–
21). Christ was supreme. All expediency was subject
to the will of Christ. The freed slave was the free slave
of Christ: but he was still a slave—a bondservant
subject to the law of Christ. To the Christian "all's
love, and all's law," just as truly as all is law and all is
love.

Law and Spirit

There is, therefore, nothing anomalous in the
paradox of law and Spirit. The Christian life is above
all else a matter of spirit. It is not a philosophy to be
debated; not an ordinance to be observed; not an ethic
to be achieved. Truth and ritual and ethic are
important, and in some sense inseparable from
Christian life and experience, but they are not of the
essence of the life in Christ. They may exist without it,
and they are in no sense essential to it. Theological
intelligence is not necessary to salvation. The pedant
who makes doctrinal instruction a necessary content
of saving faith has missed the most elementary teaching
of the New Testament, and professing wisdom, he
turns out to be what the Scriptures call a fool. The
ritualist is no wiser. In this matter circumcision is
nothing; neither is uncircumcision. Sacraments and
ordinances have their value, but neither the one nor
the other is "necessary to a cry"—and the promise is

to everyone that shall "call on the name of the Lord." Good works spring from grace, for faith without works is dead; but no logic can make that mean that grace is conditioned on works. Christianity is a life that must be imparted before it can be lived. All life is a gift, and the gift of God is eternal life. It is a matter of spirit: the Spirit of Christ indwelling the spirit of man. And if any man have not the Spirit of Christ he is none of His.

The supreme value of all life is in the quality of its spirit. The moral quality of an act is in the spirit that prompts it. Familiarity that is acceptable to a friend is an offense to a stranger. The difference between a caress and an insult is not in the act but in the spirit. Action is without morality if it be apart from questions of motive and disposition. It is the spirit that counts. In all work of the soul it is the soul that tells. Law effects nothing; certainly it makes nothing perfect. The most careful observance of technique never makes an artist, a statesman, or an orator—much less a friend, a father, or a lover. Where the spirit reigns, law is forgotten, and where the Spirit of the Lord is, there is liberty. Worship is not of rules and regulations, it is a spirit inspired by the Spirit of Life. Preaching may be perfect art and poles away from an Evangel. The power of preaching is in the demonstration of the Spirit. So it is in fellowship. Love is without law. Cupid is, of all creatures, the most erratic and incalculable; and Christian fellowship is of the breath of the four winds. From first to last, the life and work of the Christian Church are not the product of laws and rules but spring from a spirit of common life—begotten of the Spirit in Jesus Christ. The life is the life of the Spirit, and is therefore not lawless but subject to the law of the Spirit.

Law and Life

Christ's gift is a gift of life. It is called eternal life and "the life which is life indeed." Its distinctive feature is not in its duration but in its quality. It is eternal in its quality; the gift of divine life from Him who is "the same yesterday, today, and forever." Eternal life stands for fullness and fruition; life that is divine in quality and eternal in progression. It is the life of God in man. It comes by the new birth through Him who is the Spirit of Life. The same life is common to the Vine and the branches, the body and its head.

All life is subject to law. The laws of different spheres and qualities of life may not be identical, but they are analogous. In some sense the laws of life are common to all life, and the life of the believer is not without law. It needs attention or it will perish, and without cultivation there can be no progress. There are several things in which the law of the Spirit of Life follows the general order of life in other spheres. Life is inward, mysterious, and secret. It dwells somewhere at the seat of the spirit, and vitalizes personality without either absorbing or confusing it. The manifestation appears in an endless variety of forms, and yet through them all it is the same life that appears. There is unity of Spirit without a trace of uniformity in manifestation. The life of the One Spirit appears in each, according to the natural aptitudes and temperament of each, making all like Christ and no two exactly like each other.

The law of the Spirit of Life is seen also in its propagation. Life propagates by contact and cooperation. All that lives comes into being by birth, and no living thing is born of one parent. There must be mutual and complementary service. Life lives by propagation, and there is no propagation without cooperation. This is preeminently true of the law of the Spirit of Life. As the Father is dependent upon the Son for revelation, and the Son dependent upon the Spirit for both revelation and administration, so the Spirit is dependent upon the Church for evangelization. The Church is the Body of Christ, and the Holy Ghost is His Spirit. No soul enters the Kingdom of God born alone of the Spirit. There is a human agent, as well as a Divine Spirit. This goes far to explain the limitations of the Kingdom, the sterility of the Church, and the barrenness of the saints. Spiritual children come of a travailing Zion. The trouble perturbing the Church is manifested in its declining spiritual birthrate.

Space fails for extended scrutiny of the laws of protection and progress. These also are subject to law. All life is exposed to peril, and all life is given for cultivation. There must be watchfulness and nourishment, fellowship and exercise, instruction and obedience. Health must be maintained. Waste products must be shed. Carnality must be destroyed, and "the body of sin done away." There must be receptivity, cooperation, discipline, obedience. The life of the soul cannot live haphazardly. There is a law of the Spirit of Life by which spiritual life is ruled.

The Law of the Spirit of Life

The Spirit rules. Christ reigns. There are not two kings in the Kingdom of Grace. The Spirit is never called King, though He is called Lord. He is the Spirit of Life in Christ Jesus. In all things He is subject to the Son, as the Son is subject to the Father. His mission is to glorify Christ. He takes of the things of Christ and makes them known to us. He indwells the Body of Christ; and He administers the Kingdom of Christ. He calls, equips, and appoints for service. By Him, and of Him, and through Him, are all the gifts and power of the Kingdom of God. No soul is begotten of God without Him. No advance of the Kingdom is made but by Him. No victory of grace is won without Him. He is the sole source and medium of grace and power; but in all things it is "in Christ Jesus." Christ is Lord. But the Spirit of Life rules in the Kingdom of Life. He is a person in authority. To Him is committed the Body of Christ and the Kingdom of Heaven. He rules in Christ Jesus and for the Kingdom of our Lord. If we would live in the Spirit we must obey the laws of the Spirit. If we would find the power we must obey the law. We must surrender to Christ, for the Spirit cannot rule where Christ does not reign. We must yield our bodies with all their powers, for they are His temples and His instruments of righteousness. We must obey Him, for without obedience there can be neither fellowship nor cooperation. Communion means mutual understanding, mutual consecration and mutual cooperation, and it is in the communion of the Spirit of Life that we find eternal life, abiding peace, and prevailing power. The law of the Spirit of Life is found in such words as faith, prayer, truth, love, and obedience. By these the soul lives. Life is before law, but by law life is maintained and developed, and by the law of the Spirit of Life comes the fruit by which God is glorified and man is blessed. Life is often scant for want of law.

19

The Challenge of Pentecost

PENTECOST challenges the very citadel of our faith. The gift of the Spirit is the distinguishing feature of the Christian religion. It is the very soul of our faith. In His indwelling Presence is the secret of all Christian experience, and in the abiding energy of His power is the dynamic of all Christian service. The promises concerning the Spirit challenge us. The record of the Day of Pentecost challenges us. The history of the Christian Church challenges us. Do we believe in the Holy Ghost? If we do, what is the practical proof of our faith?

The Fullness of the Spirit

The blessing of Pentecost is the blessing of fullness. The symbols of wind and fire reveal the mission and quality of the Gift, but the essential truth is that they were all filled with the Holy Ghost. Fire, power, courage, and joy had their source in the fullness of the indwelling Spirit! They overflowed because they were filled to overflowing. They had already received the gift of the Spirit for salvation. In the Upper Room on the first day of the resurrection the risen Lord had breathed on them and said: "Receive ye the Holy Ghost." Pentecost was a second gift, which verified and completed the first in an infilling Presence and an overflowing power. It is the fullness that makes the difference. In a memorable passage William Arthur in *The Tongue of Fire* illustrates the difference fullness makes. "A piece of iron is dark and cold; imbued with a certain degree of heat it becomes almost burning, without any change of appearance; imbued with a still greater degree, its very appearance changes to that of solid fire, and it sets fire to whatever it touches! A piece of water without heat is solid and brittle; gently warmed, it flows; further heated, it mounts to the sky! An organ filled with the ordinary degree of air is dumb; the touch of the player can elicit but a clicking of the keys! Throw in not other air but an unsteady current of the same air, and sweet, but imperfect and uncertain, notes immediately respond to the player's touch; increase the current to a full supply, and every pipe swells with music! Such is the soul without the Holy Ghost; and such are the changes which pass upon it when it receives the Holy Ghost, and when it is filled with the Holy Ghost."

The Blessing of Fullness of the Spirit

The blessing affects the whole being. The seat of the indwelling Presence is the innermost recesses of the spiritual being, but it permeates, energizes, and controls every faculty of our nature. It is another

Incarnation of which the body is the consecrated believer. The Holy Ghost clothed Himself with the waiting disciples in the Upper Room, and He still clothes Himself with consecrated believers. He clothes Himself, and they are clothed in Him. In them He finds a Body, and in Him they find the power of spiritual expression and execution. Without confusion, without loss of personal consciousness, without change of inherent qualities, there are mutual appropriation and oneness of operation.

The effects are seen in the Apostles on the Day of Pentecost, and in every particular the experience corresponds to the promise. Jesus had said the coming of the Spirit would bring fullness of knowledge. "In that day ye shall know." Things He could not teach them they would know with certainty when the Spirit of Truth had come; and they did. There is nothing more wonderful on the Day of Pentecost than the wisdom and certainty with which they taught. Prophecy shone with new meaning, and the facts of Christ's death and resurrection were interpreted in the light of the eternal purpose of God. The Word of God became new, and the history of Christ's teaching and ministry got a new meaning. They had been dull enough before, but Pentecost changed all their outlook. The Scriptures were made luminous in the light of the Holy Ghost.

The change in their characters was even greater than the change in their knowledge. The Gospels portray these men as proud and contentious, selfish and cowardly; but the first pages of the Acts of the Apostles tell another story. Something had happened between Pilate's judgment hall and the streets of the city. Resurrection found them all shivering behind closed doors for fear of the Jews, but at Pentecost they were openly preaching Jesus and charging the rulers with His death. Pentecost transformed them. It was the fullness that made the difference between timidity and joyous daring, shivering weakness and the exultant power. They were jubilantly fearless and hilariously happy. That is the difference Pentecost always makes.

The Challenge of Fullness

How does the challenge find us? Do we measure up to the standard of the fullness of Pentecost? Is not the explanation of our confusion in the lack of it? The gift is not for the working of miraculous deeds, for there were men filled with the Holy Ghost who wrought no miracle. There is danger lest we claim more than is promised, but how do the unchallenged tests find us? What about our assurance of heavenly things? There is an end of uncertainty when the fullness of Pentecost is known.

Have we power over sin? The Spirit of Truth is the Spirit of Holiness. He sanctifies in truth. The Day of Pentecost changed carnal thought into spiritual vision, pride into humility, selfishness into love, and cowardice into courage. It changed hearts and transformed lives. Victory comes by fullness. Have we the joy of conquest over sin? Is the character of the average Christian anywhere near the standard of a Spirit-filled soul? What about the love of the world? Jesus said He was One "whom the world cannot receive." They are in irreconcilable antagonism. What has come of the doctrine of separation? If believers were filled with the Spirit, would they haunt the world's gaudy fountains and brackish springs? It is mockery to profess fullness and go about panting with thirst and gasping with vanity.

What about the power for service? Is our decline due to external difficulties or internal weakness? Think of the host of workers, the vastness and variety of their service, the earnestness and ingenuity of their labors, and the scanty result of it all. What influence has the Church upon the life of the people, and what impression does it make upon the strongholds of iniquity? What about the dearth of conversions? Pentecost brought awakening, conviction, conversions, and baptism; but the ungodly no longer speak of chapels as "converting furnaces." The gift of the Spirit is the gift of power, and the lack of power is due to the absence of His indwelling fullness. Abounding fullness overflowed in gladness, testimony, and sacrifice.

The Call to Pentecostal Fullness

There is no doubt that the one thing needful for the Church is the blessing of Pentecostal fullness. The flood would sweep away all the rubbish, fill all the dikes, and fertilize all the desert. The work of God cannot be accomplished without the fullness of the Spirit, and everywhere God waits to give His Holy Spirit to them that ask Him. It is His will that every believer should be filled with the Spirit, overflow in the power of the Spirit, and in all things prevail through the Spirit. What hinders? The blessing is for all, and for all now. The conditions are simple, unalterable, and universal. God waits to fill ordinary people with extraordinary power, and to turn a baffled faith into a rapturous conquest. How? Ask Peter and James and John! They were deeply attached and openly committed to Jesus Christ before Pentecost. They had left all for Christ's sake, but were still without Pentecost. They believed on the Lord Jesus Christ, were witnesses of His death and of His resurrection, but without Pentecost. They were workers: stewards, preachers, evangelists, workers of miracles, without Pentecost. Then they heard the Promise of the Spirit, and set themselves to claim, wait, and pray, and according to the Word the Spirit came, and they were all filled with the Holy Ghost.

20

The Way Into the Blessing

THERE are many who have not because they ask not, and there are others who ask and have not because they ask amiss. There are many who miss the Blessing because they do not seek it, but there are those who seek and do not find. There are believers who are deeply concerned about the failure and disappointment of their religious experience and their lack of effectiveness and power. They yearn for a fullness of life in Christ that never comes. They pray, and nothing happens. They seek, and somehow always miss the way. They cry unto the Lord in secret, and that which seems to come so easily to others does not come to them. They confess their need, and seek the prayers and counsel of others. They obey injunctions, repeat avowals of faith, and claim according to instructions, but the emotion passes and all is as before with the added disappointment, and another dart has been added to the quiver of the enemy. It may be as real and as easy to others as they affirm, but to them there is no answering reality to their faith, and they lose heart. They miss the blessing, but they cannot give it up. It must be there, for others have it; and it must be for them, for with God there is no respect of persons. So periodically there come a sense of hunger and a deep want of soul, and again the quest begins, and again the way is missed.

What Blessing?

Almost every day I get letters from people asking the way into the Blessing. They probably represent a great host, and I am going to try to help them, even though I must begin with the confession that my own plea for help brought me nothing but confusion. I was concerned to know what was the blessing that I knew I needed. Witnesses failed under cross-examination, and sent me books to supply what they could not give. The books were as confusing as the witnesses, but there was no doubt that they had something I had not, and I was aware that the something they had would make all the difference to me if I could find it. Somehow I was led to leave all books and interpreters and give myself up to a search of the Scriptures, believing that God would make the truth known to me.

Our Lord prayed that we might be sanctified by the truth, and I expected to find in the Scriptures the way into the Blessing. Even there the way was not easy to find, for I was seeking an explanation rather than an experience. There were no definitions, no explanations, and no interpretation of processes. My search was for a practical solution of a work wherein I had failed. I had energy and lacked power. I had ideas, and I had words of my own and other people's. But there came no convicting, converting result. The blessing I sought was power. The blessing God had for me began farther in and deeper down. Power was conditioned. The truth that sanctifies begins with cleansing of heart and motive, a life surrendered to the divine will, and a personality possessed by and filled with the Holy Spirit—and I very nearly missed the way.

The Way in the Word

The way I came is the way I know. That is why I send every seeker to the Word of God, in dependence upon the Holy Spirit of Truth. The method looks hopeless, but it works, because the Spirit is promised to guide us into all truth; and He does. In the light of the Word of God, a seeker should know what it is he seeks. The Blessing is known by many names, and it is often confused with other experiences of grace. It is known as the Pentecostal Gift of the Spirit, as Entire Sanctification, Christian Perfection, and Perfect Love, according as it is interpreted in the terms of the law, the sanctuary, or the home. The Scriptures are not written to exempt from thinking, and there are certain facts that need to be adjusted and accounted for. There are believers in the New Testament who had received the gift of the Holy Ghost and there were those who had not. There were those who were born again and yet carnal, and there were those who were sanctified. Some were addressed as "perfect," and others who had not been made "perfect." There is a "perfection" that is definite, decisive, and determinate; and there is a "perfection" that is progressive, disciplinary, and ethical; and there was an experience by which believers passed from one order to the other. It is an experience of grace in which the nature is cleansed from all sin. The carnal mind, the body of sin, is done away. That is the Bible word for what happens—sin is done away. The fullness of the indwelling Spirit sanctifies and quickens every natural faculty, and bestows gifts that are peculiarly His own. Love is made perfect, and the sanctified will is energized by divine power.

The Way of Faith

Salvation from first to last is by grace through faith. We are justified by faith, sanctified by faith, Spirit-filled by faith. There are those who think we are saved by faith and made perfect by philosophy, and there are those who imagine we are justified by faith and sanctified by works. That is why so many miss the way. This second experience of grace is the gift of God through faith unto faith. The Word of God must be received in faith. Consider the commands of God that we be holy. Search out the promises of God that we shall be holy. Pray through the prayers in the New Testament which set forth the Spirit-inspired pleadings for holiness. Have faith in God: in His Word, and in His Spirit. Where there is no faith it is useless either to ask or seek; but where faith is, prayer will prevail. Everything depends upon what you believe about God, about Jesus Christ the Saviour, and about the Holy Spirit. God meets every seeker of the Blessing with the challenge of faith: Believe ye that I am able to do this? To every man is given according to his faith. Many stumble at the question of faith. It is simple enough to those who will leave aside all disputing about faith and substitute honest obedience for subtle definitions. Faith is an attitude of mind and heart and an act of obedience to what is believed to be the truth. An honest heart never gets lost on a straight road; and the Spirit of Truth makes straight paths for the feet of every honest seeker who desires to know the truth that he may obey it. The Holy Spirit leads by the Holy Word. Obedience is the way of faith.

The children of light walk in the light, and in obedience to the light there is conscious fellowship with the God of Life, Light and Love, "and the blood of Jesus Christ His Son cleanseth us from all sin."

The test of obedience is often a trial to sense and reason, and still more to freedom and pride. The decisive battle is nearly always over some apparently trivial issue. The story of the Fall is true to the experience of life when it makes the destiny of the race turn upon the eating of an "apple." The occasion may be trivial, but the issues are momentous. It is no business of ours to go scenting idols for the burning, but the Spirit searches every honest seeker and convicts, condemns, and commands; and there is generally a bonfire when the fire of God falls. They are not things wrong in themselves that are condemned, for this Blessing is for believers, and they that are born of God do not keep sinful things in their lives. Their condemnation does not turn upon the law of right and wrong, but upon the ethical and spiritual claims of a surrendered life. So it is wide of the mark to ask, What wrong is there in these things? They are judged by the standard of Consecration and the Law of the Spirit of Life, and they must go, however profitable, however pleasant, and however right.

The Steps of Faith

Two things are plain:

(1) Pentecost is a definite work of the Spirit in believers.

(2) It is by grace through faith. Now what are the steps of faith by which the Blessing is appropriated?

The *first* step is to repent.

"And Peter said unto them, Repent ye, and be baptized every one of you in the name of Jesus Christ unto the remission of your sins; and ye shall receive the gift of the Holy Ghost" (Acts 2:38).

There is a repentance of believers as well as of sinners. When men begin to pray for the blessing of Pentecost the answer begins in conviction of sin. The things of which they are convicted, as we have said, are not transgression of the law but sins of the spirit. The things of which the believer is convicted are not in themselves sinful, but they are kept in disobedience to God's will. Things not surrendered, indulgences retained against light, possessions held for selfish ends—these must all be surrendered to the supreme authority of Christ. For until He is exalted, crowned, glorified, there can be no Pentecost.

The *second* step is to ask.

"If ye then, being evil, know how to give good gifts unto your children, how much more shall your heavenly Father give the Holy Spirit to them that ask Him" (Luke 11:13).

There must be definite asking for the specific gift. I was talking with a farmer in Lincolnshire a few years ago about prayer, and he said all the preachers he heard just now were urging people to pray and come to prayer meetings. "But," he said, "to my mind, desire has a good deal to do with praying, and praying is a slack business when desire is lacking." There must be desire that is focused into petition. "Ye have not," says James, "because ye ask not," and there are thousands of believers who have never definitely asked for the Blessing. God wants to give, but He is a God of discretion and waits to be asked. "I the Lord have spoken it, and I will do it. . . . For this, moreover, will I be inquired of by the House of Israel to do it for them."

We must be careful not to ask amiss. Nothing hinders faith so effectually as a wrong motive. "How can ye believe, which receive glory one of another, and the glory that cometh from God ye seek not?" James traces the failure of prayer to the same source: "Ye ask, and receive not, because ye ask amiss, that ye may spend it in your pleasures." The pleasures may be lawful and laudable enough, but God will not give the glory of His Son to another, and the mission of the Spirit is to glorify the Son. If the power is sought for success in Christian service merely, it will not be given. Christ must be supreme in affection and aim.

The *third* step is to receive.

When the consecration is complete, the act of faith is quite simple. "Receive ye the Holy Ghost" is the all-inclusive command. It is the word used in the Upper Room when our Lord gave them the bread that symbolized His body—"TAKE." There is a point at which asking becomes foolishness. Faith claims and takes. "Therefore I say unto you, all things whatsoever ye pray and ask for, believe that ye have received them, and ye shall have them." Take God at His word.

The *fourth* step is the continuous life of obedience.

Jesus Christ identifies faith with obedience, and in the Acts of the Apostles obedience is made the condition of receiving and retaining the Spirit. "And we are witnesses of these things; and so is the Holy Ghost, whom God hath given to them that obey Him" (Acts 5:32). Abiding fullness depends upon obedience to the ever-widening circle of illumination. The blessing of Pentecost may be lost, and it is always lost when obedience fails. The Spirit-filled must be Spirit-ruled. We are the ministers of the Spirit through whom the supply is conveyed. Those who are greatly used of God have no monopoly of the Holy Ghost; they are mighty through God because the Spirit has a monopoly of them.

Again I say this extraordinary gift is for ordinary people. All may be filled as full and as truly as the hundred and twenty on the Day of Pentecost. The conditions are the same for all: REPENT, ASK, RECEIVE, OBEY.